the Laws of Love

the
L a w s
of
L o v e

*Creating the Relationship
of Your Dreams*

CHRIS PRENTISS

Power Press

Library of Congress Control Number: 2011924445

ISBN: 978-0-943015-73-6

10 9 8 7 6 5 4 3 2

For information, address:

Power Press
6428 Meadows Court
Malibu, California 90265
Telephone: 310-392-9393
E-mail: info@PowerPressPublishing.com
Website: www.PowerPressPublishing.com

For foreign and translation rights, contact Nigel J. Yorwerth
E-mail: nigel@PublishingCoaches.com

Cover design: Nita Ybarra
Interior design: Alan Barnett Design

Note: Some of the names and details in the stories in this book have been changed to protect the privacy of those involved.

To you who seek the perfect relationship,
ever deepening, ever growing, ever broadening,
ever becoming more and more what you hope for,
long for, and strive for—may you be loved
and cherished by the one you love in
an enduring walk together along the path
you have chosen for this lifetime

Special thanks to my wife, Lyn:

*You are a treasure beyond measure,
an ever-present manifestation of how
wondrous a relationship can be when lived
in accordance with the Laws of Love.*

To the readers of The Laws of Love:

*I have now lived with my husband, Chris,
for eleven years and I want you to know that they
have been the happiest years of my life.*

~ Lyn Prentiss

CONTENTS

Author's Note

Throughout this book I have referred to your relationship partner or mate in the third person as "they" or "them" rather than "he or she" or "him or her" because it is less cumbersome and less repetitive. For instance, the phrase "You then have to live with them" can be understood as "You then have to live with him or her."

There are many words to describe a person with whom you are in a personal relationship. Again, for readability and variety, I alternate the words *partner, mate,* or *loved one* to denote the person you love and with whom you want to build your ideal relationship. If you do not consider that person to be your spouse or mate, please read that word as *partner* or another term that is applicable to your personal situation.

Acknowledgments

A special thank you once again to Nigel J. Yorwerth and Patricia Spadaro of PublishingCoaches.com. I appreciate your creativity and care, patience and persistence in helping me develop, shape, edit, publish, and promote my work. Your expertise and heartfelt support is invaluable. And thank you, Nigel, for your unwavering efforts in promoting my work, getting excellent distribution, and selling rights for my books to top foreign publishers.

I also acknowledge Carl Hartman as the person who introduced me to the brilliant concept of Safe Space in the late 1980s.

INTRODUCTION

THE PATH OF DISCOVERY

There is only one happiness in life,
to love and be loved.

~ GEORGE SAND (1804–1876)

The Laws of Love are time-tested principles for successful loving that for thousands of years have brought soul-drenching happiness and fulfilling relationships to those who have followed them. Embracing these simple truths and acting in accordance with them will empower you to shape out of the framework of your relationship, current or future, a beautiful, lasting creation that will nurture and sustain you, turn your sad days into happy days, and gladden your heart through the years. Living in harmony with these fundamental laws of life will also help you to avoid the pitfalls that beset the path of those who never give a thought to the consequences of their thoughts, words, or actions. The path to creating a wonderful relationship may at times be challenging, at times painful, but in the end always rewarding.

INTRODUCTION

THE PATH OF DISCOVERY

WHETHER YOU ARE SEEKING HELP FOR YOUR CURRENT relationship or you are seeking help in attracting a new relationship, you will find that help here. If you are currently in a troubled relationship, knowing the Laws of Love will empower you to save it—if it's worth saving. You may, in fact, be in a relationship whose usefulness has been outlived. Knowing the Laws of Love will give you the information you need to determine if you're with the right person, and it will give you the insight and the courage to end your relationship if you're not.

You may think that the course of a relationship depends on the luck of the draw or circumstances that weave their way in and out of your life. Or you may think that your happiness depends on what your partner does or does not do. The reality is that the quality of your relationship depends mainly on one thing: you.

That's not to say that your partner may not be part of the problem or may even be the entire problem, but by knowing the Laws of Love you will be able to heal your partner and bring your relationship into the light of happiness. Few relationships come to us exactly as we want them, but with the right knowledge and care we can shape them into enduring pillars of strength and beauty—relationships where great joy is experienced, great deeds are accomplished and, most importantly, great love is returned.

Once again, though, I caution you that this applies to relationships that are worth saving. Your partner may have been damaged by life, upbringing, or prior relationships to the point where your relationship is not savable. Perhaps your partner doesn't love you and doesn't want to love you, or perhaps he or she is just using you for financial reasons, emotional support, or some other hidden agenda. If after applying the Laws of Love, you discover that your partner is with you for the wrong reasons or is damaged beyond repair, you should move on with your life and find a new mate. In the words of Henry Higgins of *My Fair Lady* fame, "Throw the baggage out!"

Good Relationships Are Not an Accident

Having the relationship of your dreams is not an accident, a roll of the relationship dice. It's a result of being the kind of person who knows the right steps to take to create an enduring, fulfilling friendship with your partner. Sometimes we may meet a person who we believe is just right for us. Yet because of what we've learned about relationships and who we've become over the years, we ruin the opportunity, and what might have been a great relationship with the right person becomes another sad ending. Even the finest opportunity in the wrong hands comes to nothing.

Some twenty-five years ago, a friend of mine was sitting at my kitchen table having breakfast with me when he said, "I have the worst luck choosing women. The last nine women I have chosen to have relationships with have all turned out to be bitches."

I had to laugh at that—he had such a huge ego. "That's not true," I said. "The last nine women you chose were all sweet, gentle, loving creatures who you turned into bitches."

He angrily replied, "Who the hell do you think you're talking to?" He was very insulted, got up from the table, and stalked out of the house. I did not hear from him for four years and then he called me from Hawaii, where he was living with his wife and their one-year-old son. He said, "I'm calling to thank you and tell you that I realized that what you told me at the breakfast table that morning about how I was ruining the women in my life was correct, and I don't do that anymore." He said he was wonderfully happy with his wife and son. Today, he has three children and is still happily married.

My friend discovered what you will discover in this book: the kind of person you are at every moment is primarily responsible for the status of your relationship or your lack of a relationship. Not only that, it's also responsible for your current condition in life, your happiness or lack of it, your possessions or lack of them, and your state of well-being.

In-Formation

The world of deep, loving, rewarding, comforting relationships is a unique world, a world that very few inhabit. You will discover within this book why so few have it and why it has eluded you. You will become aware, perhaps for the first time in your life, of the information that has shaped you, that is present every minute in your life, and that is guiding and directing you and the course of your relationship. That information has been guiding you sometimes well and sometimes poorly, but always inexorably.

You currently hold in your mind ideas about how to create a relationship. Most likely you are unaware that you hold those ideas. They were formed over the years as you experienced your own relationships and observed those of others. Perhaps your ideas about how to create a good relationship were passed down to you or you learned them from something you read, heard, or saw in a movie or on television. You will try to fit your current relationship or any new relationship into the framework of those ideas. But those ideas are based largely on misinformation. If that were not true, you would already have the relationship you are seeking.

Much of what you have read, heard, and seen in the media, while it may sometimes depict the relationship you are longing for, is misleading in describing how to obtain it or does not talk about how to get it at all. It's like looking into a magazine of the lifestyles of the rich and famous and seeing their yachts, planes, mansions, and opulent standards of living but not being told how to unlock the portal to that world of affluence.

Not possessing the keys to the world of fulfilling, loving relationships will find you wandering around outside the invisible yet impregnable walls of that world, peeking into it in books, magazines, movies, television programs, your imagination, and an occasional conversation with the rare person you may meet who inhabits that world. What will allow you to enter the world of great relationships is living in accord with the simple but powerful Laws of Love. Understanding those laws and how to use them will provide you with new information—*in-formation.*

You can think of this in-formation as new ideas and concepts you will take "in" that will create a "formation" within your mind. That formation will cause you to think in a certain way about yourself and your relationship, and it will cause you to act in a certain manner with your partner.

You must come to this information prepared to remake yourself. In the eyes, heart, and mind of the one you love and who you want to love you,

you will become, in essence, a new person. As you proceed through this book, you will see how you can bring together the Laws of Love to form a ritual of conduct, a way of being, that will bring beauty and endurance to your relationship and peace and harmony to your life and the lives of those around you. Love is what you are seeking and love is what you will feel and receive when you live in harmony with these laws.

HEALING WHAT'S OUT OF BALANCE

Here's a little background on how I came to understand the Laws of Love. For many years, I've been a student of the world's most ancient writings, especially ancient Chinese philosophy. Those teachings have survived thousands of years because of their immense practical value to people, and they have much to teach us about happiness, peace, and prosperity as well as how to create meaningful and enduring relationships. I have studied these concepts for more than forty years, have put them into action in my own life, and have written about them in other books. These principles are key to healing

from the foundation up, which is how all true healing unfolds. Let me give you a parallel example.

The core concepts you will read about in this
book are also an important part of what we teach at the
Passages Addiction Cure Centers that my son Pax and
I founded. People come to our centers from all over
the world to be healed of their dependencies on drugs,
alcohol, and addictive behavior. The ones who arrive
at our door are usually in a poor state of mind. People
don't wake up in the morning feeling really good and
having everything going right in their lives and say, "I
think I'll go to Passages today." They come when the
bottom has dropped out of their lives, when they are
spinning out of control, when they have tried count-
less times to quit their addiction and failed, and when
life has become a nightmare. In our daily work, we see
every kind of relationship in every state imaginable—
from relationships between spouses or significant others that are totally supportive, loving, and caring to
relationships where spouses have just been kicked out
of their homes and are under restraining orders not to
go back or have just been served divorce papers.

At Passages we use a refreshing and innovative
approach that has revolutionized the treatment of

addiction and alcoholism. For decades, the American Medical Association has been declaring that alcoholism and addiction are diseases. Members of Alcoholics Anonymous the world over believe that those so-called diseases are incurable, giving rise to their slogans "Once an addict, always an addict" and "Once an alcoholic, always an alcoholic." At Passages, we know that alcoholism and addiction are not diseases but merely symptoms of underlying conditions that have caused and are maintaining the various addictions. Neither are drugs or alcohol the problem. The use of drugs, alcohol, and other addictive behavior is what our clients were doing *to cope* with the conditions that were the real causes of their addictions.

In other words, we do not treat our clients for alcoholism or addiction; they are only symptoms. Instead, we help our clients discover and correct the *underlying conditions* that are causing them to self-medicate, to seek relief in substances and addictive behavior. The result of this approach is almost always an addiction-free life.

The same principle applies to healing relationships that are off track. A key to making breakthroughs in any situation in need of healing is to identify what's unhealthy, what's out of balance, and then get the information that will help you to cure that condition. The way to heal your relationship is to look for the underlying conditions in yourself and in your partner that have caused your relationship to go off track and then to seek out the guidance you need to heal yourself. The Laws of Love will give you that guidance. You'll come to understand what's happening below the surface. And you'll learn how to correct what's out of balance by adjusting how you treat yourself and your loved one and by adjusting how you react to the situations that come and go in your life.

When your behavior changes, all those around you, particularly those with whom you have close relationships, will change as a result of your new behavior. That's because everyone responds to you *as you are being at every moment.* You can easily see that if you are regularly nasty to your loved one, it won't be long before cause and effect sets in and undermines your relationship. The reverse is also true: if you are unceasingly caring and loving to your loved one and act with the Laws of Love in mind, you will be deeply loved in return and your relationship will thrive. That's how Universal law works.

FIRST STEPS

Some of what you read in this book will be contrary to what you've come to believe about how to create a wonderful relationship. It may even outrage your common sense. Actually, it probably *will* outrage your common sense. That is to be expected. If it were not that way, this book would not do you much good. For the most part, what you are doing here is unlearning what you learned about relationships that is untrue and replacing it with what is true. As the Greek philosopher Antisthenes said, "The most useful piece of learning for the uses of life is to unlearn what is untrue."

When you come upon a concept in this book that outrages your common sense, before you scoff at it and discard it as unworthy, ask yourself, "Would I like that concept to be true?" Then ask yourself, "Will I give it the chance to *be* true?" Don't make the mistake of relying on your rational mind or even what you think of as your common sense, because neither one of those has brought you the relationship you want. What you think of as your common sense in regard to relationships may be based on something you have come to believe that isn't totally true or may not be true at all. Instead, take this opportunity to open your mind and heart to a new approach.

The goal you are undertaking is major and totally worthwhile. So before you go any further, get a highlighter or a pad of paper and a pen. As you read, highlight or underline sentences you feel are important to you or take notes. That way you will be able to go back through the book to see your highlighted items or review your notes so you can refresh your memory with what was most meaningful to you. Make sure you follow this important step. It is essential if you are to integrate these concepts into your life. The Laws of Love are interrelated, so you may find that several of the unfolding concepts overlap and cover some of the same ground but from a different angle. This is intentional and will help reinforce the change in outlook it takes to make the lasting changes you want.

One of the first steps on your new path is to start with a simple admission. Now, don't be alarmed; this is easy. To begin to create change, you must first admit to yourself that something about the way you've been operating has to be incorrect or you would already be getting the results you want.

For you to absorb the new information you'll be reading about here, you must first recognize and acknowledge that what you now know about creating a great relationship is, at least to some degree, not working and is based on misinformation. I'm not saying that *you* are wrong; I'm saying that *some of what you have come to believe* about creating a great relationship is wrong. I realize that's the reason you are reading this, but you must also acknowledge to yourself that you don't yet know how to do it.

So take a moment and say to yourself: "What I know about creating my perfect love relationship is in part incorrect and doesn't work." Do that now. Say it and mean it. It is not my intent to be confrontational, but it takes a certain emptying of your mind before you can put something new into it.

The Journey Ahead

Get ready now for what could be the most important journey of your life. You are now on a path of discovery that will give you the information you need to create the relationship of your dreams. More than that, it will give you insights you can use to change your entire world so it more closely resembles the world in which you would like to live.

At the conclusion of your time with this book, if I have done my job and you have done your job, you will think differently, act differently, and see the world differently. You will have re-created yourself as a different person—a happier person, a person your loved one will be overjoyed to be with, or, if you are still searching for a partner, a person who will attract and hold your newfound love. You will also achieve your goals more easily, good things will naturally flow to you, and life will be easier because you will be living in accord with Universal laws rather than in opposition to them. Here, then, are the Laws of Love.

LAW I

Universal Law Controls Everything

*To those who have conformed themselves
to The Way, The Way readily lends its power.*

~Lao Tzu (or "Old Sage," born Li Erh, sixth century bc)

Our world is governed by Universal laws, both physical and metaphysical (that is, beyond the physical). Those laws are unbreakable. They are also fixed—unchangeable. Every event, every circumstance, every situation, every manifestation of every part of nature and life unfolds only in accordance with Universal laws. By learning to live in harmony with those laws, you will discover the source of all health, all wealth, all happiness, and all joy as well as profound peace, assurance, and fulfillment in your relationships. The fact that there are laws that govern relationships should be a great comfort to you because once you know those laws, you can completely depend on them in every situation to accomplish your relationship goals.

LAW I

UNIVERSAL LAW
CONTROLS EVERYTHING

THE LAWS OF THE UNIVERSE WERE IN EFFECT BEFORE you were born, they are in effect now, and they will remain in effect long after the physical form you're in now has been transformed and you have moved on in your journey through time and space. Universal laws are in action all around us and in us. In a vacuum, light travels 186,282.397 miles in one second—no more, no less. It's a law of the Universe. You can depend on it.

Sir Isaac Newton, born in 1642, formulated the idea of gravity while sitting under an apple tree and seeing an apple fall to the ground. The short version of his concept is that every object in the universe exerts a physical attraction on every other object. The force of the attraction depends on the mass of the object and its distance from other objects. The smaller the mass of the object and the greater the distance from other objects, the less will be the attraction. The apple is attracting the earth to it and the earth is attracting the apple to it by virtue of the same gravitational force. The reason the apple falls to the earth instead of the earth rising to the apple is because the mass of the apple is very small compared to the mass of the earth. That's a Universal Law, a law that has been represented in a precise scientific formula.

Day after day, year after year, Earth rotates around the sun at 67,000 miles per hour, give or take a few miles per hour, and it is spinning around its own axis at just over 1,000 miles per hour. Our moon travels at a speed of 2,288 miles per hour as it travels around the earth in an ellipse (an oblong figure) that is 1,423,000 miles around. Everything moves in accord with fixed Universal laws.

You discovered both physical and metaphysical laws through trial and error. As a child, if you thought you could walk through a tree, you bumped your nose. If you thought you could fly and you jumped from a high place, the resultant pain as you crashed to the ground convinced you otherwise. You learned from trying to break physical laws just how unbreakable those laws were and always will be.

You learned about metaphysical laws in much the same way. If you treated your friends badly, you lost them as friends. If you lied a lot, no one trusted you. If you were thoughtful, loyal, and considerate, you were well liked.

Perfect Order

Everything that happens—all events, all situations, and all changes—are a result of a Universal law manifesting itself. Some scientists who believe in chaos don't agree with that. They point to a sunset as an example and say, "That's an example of chaos," meaning a state of utter confusion or disorder with the atoms of the sunset occurring without fixed order or control. Yet that is nonsense, as every atom in every sunset is completely controlled by Universal laws acting upon it, such as the laws of gravity and electromagnetism.

Chaos means that anything can occur at any time without fixed laws governing the occurrences. However, "anything" *does not happen.* Here's an example. According to our best scientific evidence, the Universe has been in its current state for approximately

13.73 billion years, give or take 120 million years or so. If chaos were part of the Universal scheme and anything could happen at any time, surely in the last 13.73 billion years, the Universe would have destructed. But that has not happened; it continues on and on. Therefore, we must rule out chaos. And if we do that, what's left is perfect order. From all these facts and many more, I conclude, and hopefully you will too, that we are part of a Universe where perfect order prevails and everything happens *only* in accordance with Universal law.

Do you believe in chaos—in random, uncontrolled events, in the idea that anything can happen at any time without fixed laws governing it? If you believe that, you will always be in a state of fear, not knowing what will happen from one moment to the next. The fear might be small, but it is there. That fear results in a lack of security and a feeling of mistrust.

Learning about the Laws of Love will help free you from that fear because you can absolutely depend on these laws. The Laws of Love are as unerring and as unbreakable as the laws that govern the speed of light and the rate of increase in the speed of falling objects. If we live in accordance with the Laws of Love, we create beautiful and satisfying relationships. If we don't, we're just like the people who hurt themselves by thinking that they can walk through trees or that they can jump from a high place and fly. Just as you can boil water by knowing the Universal law that at sea level fresh water boils when it reaches 212 degrees Fahrenheit, so by discovering and working with the Laws of Love, you'll know how to make your relationship reach its boiling point. (Of course, you don't want to keep it there because, for the long run, a gentle simmer is best!)

This first Law of Love—that Universal law controls everything, even your relationships—sets the stage for the rest of the laws. Remember as you read what follows that the path to a magnificent relationship is always directly in front of you. You may take the first step upon it at any time and wonderfully transform your circumstances. The path that leads to unhappiness in your relationships, the path that ignores the Laws of Love, is also always directly in front of you. At each step of your way, you must choose between those two paths. The beginning of one is always the ending of the other. Your relationship is entirely in your own hands, and everything is possible.

LAW 2

Everything Is in a State of Constant Change

You cannot step twice into the same river,
for other waters are ever flowing on to you.

~ HERACLITUS OF EPHESUS (540 BC – 480 BC)

The Universal Law of Change provides that *everything* in the Universe will be forever in a state of constant change—except the laws of the Universe, which always remain fixed. Life is like a river: nothing is ever the same, even for an instant. As for your relationship, it too is in a constant state of change, always improving or deteriorating as the days of your relationship unfold. What that means is that you must be ever vigilant so that as the inevitable changes occur, you react in a way that is in harmony with the Laws of Love rather than haphazardly, without taking the laws into consideration. What's even better is to be the architect of the changes in your relationship, intentionally bringing about the changes that will create the relationship you visualize in your best dream. In either case, by acting in accordance with Universal laws, you'll always bring about the best results in your relationship.

LAW 2

EVERYTHING IS IN A
STATE OF CONSTANT CHANGE

YOUR LIFE IS IN A STATE OF CONTINUAL EVOLUTION. The world's most ancient and revered traditions tell us that as part of this natural process of growth, we will be tempered in the fire of life. It is an eternal law of life that we must all pass through the fire, for that is where strength is gained, endurance enhanced, and the secrets of our hearts revealed to us. The fire of life is the Universal force that is constantly shaping us. As the ancient Chinese text called the I Ching (literally "Book of Changes") tells us, "The Universe endlessly shapes and changes us until we each find our true nature and then keeps us in tune with the Great Harmony."

Life's tempering and altering process often takes the form of adversity, and, as far as outward appearances are concerned, seems to be working against us when it is actually working for us. In other words, one way the Universe helps you grow and keeps you in "great harmony" is to present you with challenging situations and events.

You know the old saying that a chain is only as strong as its weakest link. Well, you're only as strong as your area of greatest weakness. The challenges and changes you meet are, in effect, hand delivered to you by a generous, loving Universe for the purpose of making you stronger and wiser. Circumstances may look like problems, feel like problems, and seem like problems, but that's just one point of view. Once you learn to look at your problems as "workout situations," they take on a whole new aspect. I call them "workout situations" because they are just that: situations you can "work out on" so that you can gain strength and understanding. After you have done that, the circumstances are of no further use to you and they pass out of your life, not to return, as long as you keep aware of what you learned and don't choose to act in opposition to what you learned.

When you are living in accord with Universal laws, you're safe and life unfolds beautifully, pleasantly, and happily. In fact, that is how you can determine if you are following the Universal laws. The moment you begin working in opposition to Universal laws, you get an unpleasant result that will let you know you've stepped off the Path or that a certain area of your life needs more strengthening. I capitalized the word *Path* here to draw your attention to its importance. All of life is on this Path of evolution.

These same principles are acting in your relationships. Events, situations, and people change, and along the way of those changing circumstances you may face what look like and feel like obstacles and hardships. To see each of those events and situations for what they are—opportunities for growth and improvement—is essential for the creation and maintenance of a loving relationship.

THE RHYTHM OF YOUR LOVE

Just as situations in your life and in your relationships will change, so will your individual needs and the needs of your partner. For your relationship to prosper, you must both be aware of those changes and be ready to respond in a way that always strengthens your relationship. You may have heard the following analogy before, but it's worth revisiting. A relationship is like a garden. To create a condition that will cause your plants to thrive and produce abundantly, you must weed, water, fertilize, and care for the plants in your garden. You must also know about the special needs of the plants you're caring for. Some need more or less light than others, some need more or less water than others, and some need special fertilizers.

To create a wonderful, long-lasting, fruitful relationship, a relationship where love is the guiding principle, you must create a favorable condition within which your relationship will thrive and endure. And to do that, you must know about the special needs of your partner. Each of us is different and has different needs. In addition, our needs change over the course of our relationship. When you are committed to an enduring relationship with someone, you aren't simply concerned about having *your* needs met. You also go out of your way to care for your loved one, being aware of and adaptable to their changing needs.

It is not enough to say that you will treat your partner in the same fashion you would like to be treated. Your partner may require care beyond what you need. So in nurturing a relationship, it is important for you to find out what the needs of your loved one are and to provide for them. That process doesn't happen just once; it happens over and over again. It's part of the rhythm of your shared love. As Confucius said, "They must often change who would be constant in happiness or wisdom."

So a key to working with the Law of Change in your relationship is flexibility. *To remain inflexible when all else is changing is to invite disaster*. It is paramount to the success of your relationship that you set a firm course and that you be stable enough in your character not to waver with every argument or disturbance. It is equally essential, however, that you be aware of changing conditions and be open and flexible enough in your thinking to change with changing conditions.

Maintaining rigidity leads to failure. Remaining flexible leads to success. The following saying, often misattributed to Darwin, conveys the same thing in another way: "It is not the strongest of the species that survives, nor the most intelligent, but the one most responsive to change." Of course, there are changes that can occur in a relationship that are not acceptable, things such as cheating, lying, physical abuse, prolonged alcohol or drug abuse, and other addictive behavior. If those habits are permitted, disaster is almost sure to follow. Later, I'll write more about what I call "deal breakers," situations where you should end the relationship and move on.

The Goal of Endurance

When you are serious about your relationship, then the preservation of the relationship itself—the life-long love and support you share—will always be more important to you than the changes, disturbances, and disagreements that will inevitably occur. What allows a partnership to survive the difficulties, failures, successes, and changes that all relationships experience as part of the human condition is the all-important trait of endurance. We will revisit this in more detail later, but here are a few examples to introduce this key concept.

Let's say that you receive an excellent job offer that will require you to be away from your loved one for several months. The offer is exceptional with a substantial sum of money, great benefits, and great prestige for you. Your mate objects to your taking the job because it will separate the two of you and put a strain on the relationship. What do you do?

The answer is absolutely clear: you do not take the job. And you put it aside willingly, gladly, and with a song in your heart, knowing that you have chosen love as your lodestar. A lodestar is an unfailing, guiding light that you can depend upon to always lead you in the right course of action. The heart of the matter is that you must choose to make the relationship more important than the job opportunity. *If you would have your relationship endure, fix your mind on an end that endures.* Focus on the continuation of your relationship.

What if your partner wants you both to join a hiking group on weekends rather than spending time with the same circle of friends you've been seeing for years? What if your partner is really adamant about it? Will you get angry or upset? Will you absolutely refuse to do it, or will you agree to change your opinion and your weekend pastime to try something new? Will you give yourself and your partner the freedom to grow and experiment, or will you risk your relationship? Again, the heart of the matter is that you must choose to make the relationship more important than resisting your partner's idea to join a hiking group.

The same applies to arguments. If you allow disagreements and arguments to escalate, you are making the bone of contention of whatever you are heatedly arguing about more important than your relationship. Whatever you are arguing about is more important than the relationship *only if you make it so.* Here is the rule: don't make what your partner does or says more important than your partner.

THE POWER OF
FLEXIBILITY AND ADAPTABILITY

Be ever soft and pliable like a reed,
not hard and unbending like a cedar.

~ THE TALMUD (CA. 200 CE, 500 CE)

From this point on, you will find after each of the chapters in this book questions for self-reflection and ideas for taking your next steps in creating your ideal relationship. To reflect on the Law of Change and the power of flexibility and adaptability, think about the following questions. Please answer aloud if you are alone or in your mind if you are not alone.

~ How flexible am I in responding to the needs and desires of my partner?

~ Do I always demand that things happen the way I want them to in our relationship?

~ What is an example of a time when I did not adapt well to a change within a relationship? What was the result?

~ What is an example of a time when I did adapt well to a change within my relationship? How did I adapt and what was the result?

~ What changes are happening in my relationship right now?

~ What specific steps can I take to be flexible and adapt to these changes in order to preserve my relationship or make it better?

~ If I am searching for a mate, will I promise myself to be adaptable when I find what I am seeking?

LAW 3

YOUR PHILOSOPHY
DETERMINES THE QUALITY
OF YOUR RELATIONSHIP

Man is made by his belief.
As he believes, so he is.

~ The Bhagavad Gita (ca. 500 bc)

We all have a personal philosophy. Your personal philosophy is what you believe to be true about the world and how it works. Your philosophy causes you to respond to events in a particular manner, and that, in turn, determines how events and circumstances affect you and how you affect them. You may not be aware of the power of your philosophy to shape your life, of how it guides your actions and is responsible for the choices you have made in your life, but your personal philosophy is working full time in your life every day, all day. If you change your philosophy, your life will change, your relationship will change, and everything around you will change as it responds to your new philosophy.

LAW 3

YOUR PHILOSOPHY
DETERMINES THE QUALITY
OF YOUR RELATIONSHIP

OVER TIME, YOU HAVE BEEN FASHIONED INTO THE person you are by parents, teachers, friends, the media, books you have read, films you have seen, and your personal experiences. Your perception of the world and the way you see yourself in it has created within your mind certain concepts, which, when taken together, form your philosophy. Your philosophy was largely created without your awareness that it was happening.

The philosophy you developed over the years since you were born is primarily responsible for what your life is like today as you read this. It is responsible for who you are and what you have. Acting on the basis of your philosophy is also responsible for the state of your current relationship or lack of one. Quite simply, the opinions you have formed about how to have a wonderful relationship are what guide your actions and reactions today.

In short, you are the one who is creating both the good and the bad aspects of your relationship and of your life by your choices, which are based on what you believe—your philosophy. As Eleanor Roosevelt said, "One's philosophy is not best expressed in words; it is expressed in the choices one makes.... In the long run, we shape our lives and we shape ourselves."

What You Believe

The old saying "The more you do of what you've done, the more you'll get of what you have" has much merit. It's a simple working formula: if who you are and what you have—in your relationships, at home, or on the job—are what you want, that's perfect; keep doing what you've been doing and you'll get more of it. However, if who you are and what you have is less than or different than what you want, you'll have to make some basic changes. You can't produce different results than you are now experiencing in your relationship or in your life without changing what you've been doing.

To accomplish different results, you will have to change something in the way you think. You will have to reinvent the way you see your world. I refer to it as "your" world, because each of us lives in a different world. Of course we all live on planet Earth, we all have our ups and downs, and we all need food, clothing, and shelter. But your childhood was different from anyone else's, your parents or lack of them was different, your experiences were different, your traumas were different, your health history was different, your schooling was different, your challenges were different, the life lessons you learned were different, your thoughts were different, and your conclusions were different.

As a result, your philosophy—your belief in how the world works—is different. Even if the differences were small, those small differences make *all* the difference. That means that what is true for someone else may not be true for you, and probably isn't. What works for another may not work for you, and probably doesn't. The Laws of Love work for everyone, but you must apply them in your own way and to your own circumstances. The changes you need to make in reinventing your world will be specific to you.

Here are a few examples of beliefs that make up a philosophy (some of these examples may be part of your own philosophy, what you believe to be true): "It's a dog-eat-dog world." "Into every life some rain must fall." "Bad things happen to good people." "Lasting happiness isn't really possible." Or perhaps you believe "Things in my life always turn out for the best" or "Every cloud has a silver lining" or "I am in charge of the course of my life."

What about your relationship? As I said, your personal philosophy guides what you believe about relationships too. It determines what you think about the nature of relationships and how to create great relationships, and whether you think that's even possible. Your personal philosophy also determines what you think you deserve in a relationship. In turn, every one of your ideas and beliefs shape what your relationships become.

You may, for example, hold some of these beliefs about relationships: "People generally can't be trusted." "You've got to take the bitter with the sweet." "I don't really deserve the perfect relationship." "My happiness depends on the person I marry." "You have to be really lucky to have a great relationship." "I'm not a lucky person." Or perhaps your beliefs are along these lines: "I expect good things to come my way." "I can always see goodness in people." "I can take every situation, no matter how bad it seems, and turn it into good fortune." "Every ending contains a new beginning, a new opportunity." "How I act and react determines the quality of my relationships." "I'm a good person and I deserve to be loved."

The Patterns We Are Taught

I, too, had my personal philosophy formed by my early experiences. I've told this story about my mother in some of my other books, but it's important to include at least part of it here to show you how what we learn from the key people in our lives does indeed influence our own relationships later in life—unless we consciously do something to retrain ourselves. My story is somewhat dramatic, but we all pick up patterns and beliefs from those who raised us, beliefs we're often not aware of.

My mother, Bea, was a lawless woman who had learned to survive by her wits. (I was never permitted to call her mom or mother, only Bea.) When I was three-and-a-half, one of the first lessons Bea taught me, and that had a hold on me over the next twenty years, was "Never tell the truth." She said, "Only fools tell the truth." And she followed it up with "Never tell the truth when a good lie will suffice."

One of her lessons in lying was "a good liar has to have a good memory." So I memorized endless poems, long ones, to improve my memory. And she said if I was ever caught in a lie, I should never admit to it, even if I was caught red-handed. She would tell me stories of people who had been accused of telling a lie and had never owned up to it, and how, after a time, those who had been told the lie were never 100 percent sure whether or not they had been lied to.

Bea was born in New York City in 1900. Her father was a longshoreman who worked on the docks, and her mother was a stay-at-home mom who took care of Bea, her two sisters, and her brother. They were very poor. When Bea was fifteen, she was raped by an older man, became pregnant, and the older man was forced to marry her. They hated each other, and Bea reported that he delighted in tormenting her. She sewed buttons on shirts, earning fifty cents a day, to get spending money and pined for the day she could get out of the marriage. When she finally got out of the marriage three years later, she was as tough and hard as a diamond. She was also totally unforgiving, never forgetting a wrongdoing and waiting patiently to pay back every wrong done to her. I saw her wait twenty-four years to pay someone back for having wronged her and it kept her happy for months. As for the man who raped her, she caused him endless misery until the day he died.

In the roaring twenties, Bea was in her twenties. She was poor and learned to live by her wits in a wild and lawless element of New York City. She turned to a life of crime, and by the time she was twenty-one she ran a stolen-car ring in New Jersey and had a gang of con artists working for her in New York City. Prohibition began in 1920 and Bea was immediately on the scene running whiskey to the speakeasies, the thousands of illegal clubs, operating in New York City. She became successful living outside the law and was determined that I, too, should become successful in the same way.

By the time I was four, Bea had taught me to shoplift, and I was praised warmly for my little successes. She didn't need to shoplift; she just loved doing it. A single parent, she taught me to survive by any means, and I learned well. She told me to never trust anyone, particularly women, who were only out for what they could get from me. My early business career was characterized by deceit, trickery, and fraud. No one with whom I had business dealings was safe. I even cheated my friends. It was great fun, and I made considerable money doing it. In the evening, Bea and I would sit and talk about the cheating and conniving we had done, and we shared many a good laugh over our trickery.

YOU CREATE YOUR FUTURE
MOMENT BY MOMENT

You can imagine what my relationships at that time were like under the influence of Bea. I always deceived my girlfriends about my underhanded activities. I lied to them even about mundane things, and I cheated on them and thought nothing of it. I actually loved doing it, not realizing I was destroying any chance for a loving, trusting relationship. I would carry on several relationships at the same time, keeping each one unaware of the others. I married when I was twenty-one, but the relationship had zero chance of success given my abundant character flaws. When my wife gave birth to our son, I was out at a club with two women. The marriage ended a year or so later when my wife caught me leaving a restaurant in the company of one of my girlfriends.

What finally saved me from a life of crime and deceit was my appetite for reading. I read every day, mostly fiction, and through those books I began to perceive a different way of life. I read of courage, valor, integrity, and a life lived as a hero, and I was powerfully drawn to such a life.

One day, when I was twenty-three, I sat at my kitchen table and mentally looked at the shambles I had made of my life. Sure, I had made some money, had a real estate office in my own building, had built houses, created subdivisions, and sold land, but I hadn't been able to hold on to any of it. I had no real friends, my reputation was terrible, and everyone was afraid of me because I was so deceitful. I was a failure as a husband, a father, a friend, a businessman—and as a man; I had hurt so many people.

At that moment, I realized that Bea, that warm-hearted, generous, fun-loving, protective mother whom I loved and who loved me, had programmed me totally in the wrong direction. Following the course she had set for me, I would surely wind up in prison, friendless, alone, and certainly without a loving relationship. I was overwhelmed by remorse, and I made a decision to discover the way to real success, real happiness, real love, real inner peace, and lasting prosperity.

I tried for several years to turn my life around where I lived in New Jersey, but Bea's influence was too strong. So in 1965, at the age of twenty-nine, I drove to California, determined to become the man I dreamed of being. When I told Bea of my plan to change my life to one of honor and integrity, her comment was "What a jerk!" She had nothing but scorn for that way of life.

Since 1965, I have been searching the world for the wisdom that has sustained people and brought them great success, true love, abundant prosperity, and lasting happiness. My search took me to other countries, and I read the world's most ancient writings that had been handed down through thousands of years to this day. One book in particular, the I Ching, the five-thousand-year-old book of wisdom from China, was of immense value to me. In the writings of that book and others, I discovered a clear path that led to the wonderful gifts I sought. I also learned about the laws of the Universe—and the Laws of Love.

One of the most important lessons I learned over those years is that I am a participant in creating my future, moment by moment, as I respond to the events of my life. That's true for you as well.

Being the way you are at every moment, living your life according to your personal philosophy, has brought you to this point in your life. Changing your philosophy will change everything. In essence, our thoughts produce our actions, which, in accord with Universal law, produce effects. The effects become, for us, the future.

WHAT ARE YOUR EXPECTATIONS?

Your expectations and intentions are a powerful part of your philosophy. You create your world by your expectations. It works like this: Thinking the world a selfish place, you find selfishness. Selfishness is what you expect, what you look for, and, consequently, what you find. Having found it, and seeing your beliefs confirmed, you say to yourself, "I knew it!" Thinking the world a generous place, you find generosity. Believing yourself capable, you set out toward accomplishment; believing yourself incapable, you fail to even begin and therefore you seldom succeed in reaching your goals.

When you imagine yourself as a failure or as having insurmountable problems in your relationships or any part of your life, you think failure, act failure, and produce failure. "Moment by moment, we mold our futures," ancient Chinese wisdom tells us. "Using your imagination, you sow the seeds of your success, the seeds of your failure."

People who have voluntarily ended their lives did so for only one reason: they were hopeless, and they used their imaginations to envision a dismal future without end. Other people in the same conditions and circumstances used their imaginations to envision hope. They saw the possibility of bright, happy, prosperous futures and they survived, they were happy, and they prospered in the bright futures they imagined.

What are your relationship expectations? Do you believe that you can have a truly loving and fulfilling relationship? If the relationships you saw and experienced while growing up made you believe that good relationships are not possible, challenge that belief now by opening to the possibility that it can be different for you. That's not just a possibility; it's the truth. You are far more powerful than you believe, and everything you conceive of is within your grasp.

THE POWER OF
YOUR THOUGHTS AND EXPECTATIONS

Whatever the mind can conceive and believe, the mind can achieve.... Your only limitations are those which you set up in your own mind or permit others to set up for you.

~ NAPOLEON HILL (1883–1970)

If you do not have the great relationship you desire, or if you are not happy most of the time, then you must change your personal philosophy. Take a moment now and think about what you learned about relationships as you were growing up and how that has helped mold your personal philosophy. Please answer each of the following questions aloud if you are alone or in your mind if you are not alone.

~ What kind of relationships did my parents or the important people in my life have?

~ How did they interact in their relationships?

~ What did their interactions and beliefs teach me about relationships?

~ What do I now believe about relationships?

~ Do I believe a fulfilling, satisfying relationship is possible for me?

~ Do I believe that I deserve a wonderful relationship?

No matter what your answers to the above questions are, by following the Laws of Love you can achieve the relationship of your dreams. One step you can take right now to reset your relationship beliefs is to begin to expect that it *is* possible to create the relationship you want, no matter what kind of relationships you or your parents or role models had. If you knew that you were creating the world by your thoughts, beliefs, and expectations, wouldn't you create thoughts, beliefs, and expectations that would lead you to the realization of your fondest dreams?

Did you ever stop to think about how things are made? That includes everything that was ever made. The steps begin with someone imagining the object to be made. Then that person might have drawn the object, then perhaps developed a prototype, and then created the actual object. In every case, it always began *with someone imagining the object to be made.* That's how we create things, including relationships.

This is the time for you to recall your unrealized dreams of the relationship you want and to hold them clearly in your mind. *Just by bringing them to mind, you have already started them on their way into the physical realm.* Of course, it will take more than that to make those dreams a reality. You'll read more about this under Law 7, but imagining what you want is the starting point.

~ Find a comfortable place and sit quietly for five minutes.

~ Close your eyes and imagine what you want your relationship to look like, feel like, and be like. In that perfect relationship, how will you treat your loved one and how will he or she treat you? What kind of person do you want in your life? And what kind of qualities will *you* work on developing so that kind of person will be attracted to you?

~ Do this every day for ten days. You can continue this beyond ten days if you wish and you may spend more than five minutes doing this each day.

~ Write down your answers to the questions above and look at what you've written every day. You can make changes in your answers if you like.

You are in charge of your imagination. By using it to imagine a wonderful relationship and a brilliant future for yourself, and by acting on that basis, it will follow unerringly that, for you, *it will be so*.

LAW 4

Relationships Only
Thrive in Safe Space

We find rest in those we love,
and we provide a resting place
in ourselves for those who love us.

~ BERNARD OF CLAIRVAUX (1090–1153)

Your relationship thrives, withers, lives, or dies in an environment. If the environment in which your relationship lives is harsh and unforgiving, a place where sarcasm, degradation, and anger is present and where forgiveness, thoughtfulness, and love are in short supply, your relationship will wither and die...painfully. It will die just as a garden dies without water, nutrients, and light. Your generosity, understanding, good nature, supportive attitude, gentleness, and knowledge of the Laws of Love are the nutrients and the bonds of a strong, endearing, and enduring relationship. Blended together, they create the environment for a successful relationship: Safe Space.

LAW 4

RELATIONSHIPS ONLY THRIVE IN SAFE SPACE

HERE IS THE HEART OF THE LAW OF LOVE REGARDING Safe Space: *in your eyes, your partner cannot make a mistake or do anything wrong.* That is the ultimate condition of Safe Space. That doesn't mean your partner will not make mistakes, do things you don't agree with, or do things that are hurtful to you or someone you care about. What it means is that you will treat their action as if nothing wrong was done, as if what happened is fine with you.

You will not be harsh, hurtful, sarcastic, degrading, or even somewhat put off by what happened. You will keep in mind as you respond that you are talking to someone you want to love you completely, warmly, and sincerely. You are talking to someone you want to spend the rest of your life with. If you were able to choose how your partner would treat you, wouldn't you want to be treated gently, lovingly, and with great tenderness and complete consideration no matter what you were to do?

The degree to which you provide Safe Space for your loved one is the same degree to which your relationship will blossom and the same degree to which you will find the love you seek in the eyes and heart of the one you love. The degree to which you fail to provide Safe Space is the same degree to which your relationship will diminish, tarnish, and die. If you do not offer a haven of Safe Space, your mate may become afraid of you and afraid to make mistakes, which will surely cause those mistakes to occur. If you would exist in that rarified world of relationship heaven where only a few have entered and even fewer have remained, you must *fully* embrace the condition of Safe Space.

When you live by the law that relationships only thrive in Safe Space, you do not become upset or angry with your partner over hurtful events caused by them because you know that, speaking in today's vernacular, you've got to cut them some slack—in fact, total slack—if you want to be loved. Creating Safe Space requires nothing less than becoming the kind of person who looks with perfect equanimity on the shortcomings of your loved one—the kind of person who sees the seeming mistakes, omissions, blunders, failures, and even the intentional hurts and transgressions and makes them all okay.

Making Your Love Felt

At this point, there will most likely arise in your mind a myriad of examples in your current or past relationships that you can point to and say, "Well, what about this or that—am I supposed to just overlook those things? Am I supposed to say, 'Okay honey, it's alright that you continue to lie to me." Or "Don't worry, dear, about not paying the bills on time, month after month, and ruining our credit. I understand you were busy with your friends and I love you just the same."

Lying is not okay. Ruining your credit is not okay. Driving recklessly is not okay. Being disrespectful or nasty to you is not okay. Neglecting important things is not okay. Cooperation is not a sentiment; it is an economic necessity. If those transgressions and things like them continue despite your best efforts to help your partner correct them, they enter into the domain of "deal breakers."

Before the above examples turn into deal breakers, when they are still in the annoying stage but have not become intolerable, it's essential that you create Safe Space for your partner so you do not wind up appearing uncaring or difficult or making them feel as if you don't love them. How you treat your partner during those occurrences will determine the degree of love and respect you will receive from your partner.

In the universal sense of the word, all events are part of the perfection of the unfolding Universe, part of your process of growth. By acting in accord with that truth and carefully adhering to what you have just read about Safe Space, your partner will revere you, love you, cling to you, and be forever grateful to you for being the loving, compassionate, and understanding person they have always dreamed of and longed for, either consciously or subconsciously. Your loved one will speak about you and think about you in the highest terms of endearment. You will have earned their love.

Providing Safe Space for another is, in reality, an act of complete selfishness. What you are after is to be totally loved by the one you love. You are, in fact, the direct beneficiary of your creation of Safe Space. First, you get to live with and experience the joy and love of someone who is free to grow and expand in the Safe Space you have created. Second, you get to experience what it's like to live with someone who is not afraid of doing the wrong thing. That leaves you and your partner free to experiment as you move through life and removes fear from your relationship. And third, because your mate has experienced what it is like to live with a person who is generous and compassionate, they will therefore want to provide you with the same Safe Space you have provided them. As my wife, Lyn, says, "Partnerships allow you to love yourself and life through another."

To the extent that you have created Safe Space, your partner will have perfect trust in you. Your partner will "know" you—know you to be in love with them and know that they can trust you to be loving in response to any action they take, even actions that would seem to the world to be mistakes, bad judgment, or even intentional transgressions.

Removing Fear from Your Relationship

Here's an example of how Safe Space manifests itself in a perfect relationship environment. Say your spouse takes the new car out to run an errand and smashes it. When you are committed to Safe Space in your relationship, your response will be: "As long as you're safe, that's all I really care about. I hope you're not upset by it. I want you to know that I love you, and that you are my treasure. I was so worried about damaging our new car, and now I realize that the only thing that is important is that you are safe and sound. Cars are replaceable—you're not!"

How do you think your spouse will respond to that? I know how I would respond. I would feel a surge of love and gratitude for being in the presence of someone who truly loves me, who thinks far more of me than of the banged-up car, whose first and main concern is my well-being. Wouldn't you feel the same?

Here's another example of how to create Safe Space in your relationship. Say you arrive at the airport, only to discover that your partner forgot to bring his or her driver's license or passport as identification. Your response: "No problem, honey. We're obviously not supposed to be on that flight. Since we can't fly until tomorrow, let's have a special celebration tonight to make the most of this unexpected bonus time. I'm actually glad we missed the flight. Something good will come of it. Do you know, I may have forgotten to lock the back door. This will give me a chance to check on it."

Then, all during the rest of that day, find reasons to feel good about having missed the flight. Make statements such as these: "It would take a heck of a lot more than that for me to ever be angry with you. You're such a perfect partner for me, and I don't want you to feel uncomfortable, even in the slightest, for anything you do." "Do you know, if we hadn't missed that flight, we might never have discovered this great restaurant." "If we had made that flight, you wouldn't have gotten that important phone call from work."

Safe Space relieves apprehension on the part of your loved one. We all know what it feels like when we know we are going to be scolded or punished for having done something wrong. *Those feelings should be absent in your relationship.* Making everything your partner does okay with you will remove most of what causes dissension in relationships. There's really nothing quite like Safe Space for creating and maintaining a wonderful, loving, stress-free relationship.

Don't forget about yourself too. Remember to create Safe Space for yourself as well. Don't needlessly beat yourself up over things you've done that you wish you hadn't. Be patient with yourself. Give yourself the right to be happy with yourself and your actions. Many a life has been ruined because of long-term feelings of guilt, regrets about missed opportunities, and the whole world of coulda, woulda, shoulda.

To Truly See, Look with Your Heart

Communication is probably the single most important aspect of creating an enduring relationship. To be able to communicate effectively, you have to create a condition where the communication can freely take place, a safe atmosphere for you and your partner to share ideas, thoughts, and concerns. Within that safe atmosphere, each of you can openly speak to the other without fear of incurring anger, criticism, or reprisal.

For example, if your partner tells you something in confidence and a week later you use it against your partner, chances are you will have destroyed the safe atmosphere where confidences can be shared, and open communication will become difficult, if not impossible. Similarly, if your partner tells you something personal and you become angry or critical, you have most likely destroyed the safe atmosphere wherein each of you can exchange those types of confidences.

How you react to your partner in your communications is based on how you listen and how you see, both of which are completely subjective. It is one thing to see with your eyes; but to truly see, you must look with your heart. When you see with your physical eyes, you actually do not see objects. You see the light rays that bounce off the objects. The rays of light that enter your eye stimulate the rods and cones in your retina and, in turn, create electrical impulses that travel along the optic nerve system to the brain. Your brain receives those impulses and forms a picture, which you then interpret. It is in the interpretation that the use of your heart comes into play.

Interpreting what you see by seeing with your heart is what allows you to feel compassion for your partner's suffering, joy for your partner's happiness, concern for your partner's need. It is in seeing and listening with your heart that you learn to forgive, to make allowances for yourself and your mate, to withhold judgment, and to refrain from jumping to conclusions that may be in error. It is in seeing and listening with your heart that you learn to love as you properly should—with a heart full of kindness, love, and care.

In communication, words cannot completely express our thoughts. Ten people may describe a horse, but that doesn't tell us exactly what a horse *is*. Feelings are particularly difficult to convey in words. You can say, "I love you," but that means something different to each of us. You have the best chance of communicating your thoughts if you are sincere and speak from your heart, without hidden intent.

In communication, intent is the key word. If you intend to speak truthfully, without flattery or trickery, without any intent to deceive, and with sincere intent to communicate your love, you have the best chance of communicating your true thoughts and not being misunderstood. It's a huge benefit to learn to *love the ring of words that tell the truth*, for in that love lies your best chance of being understood and believed.

Another key to creating Safe Space in communication is to make space to listen to what your partner says to you. The Universe communicates itself to us in many ways, and sometimes it is through the words of others that you learn what you need to know. Being open to what others have to say, even encouraging them to give you feedback, is especially key in your relationships. It is more important to listen to others than to be always speaking, for in that way you learn what there is to know.

Beware of subtly shutting down the people in your life by acting as if you are a know-it-all. A person who speaks as if he knows everything soon drives away his listeners. If you act the know-it-all, others may refrain from talking to you and you won't get the message they could have given you—a message that could mean the difference between success and failure in a relationship. In order to create Safe Space for communication, you should be easy to talk to and grateful for new information.

The challenge, of course, comes when what you receive from others is contradictory to your own thoughts and expectations. When that's the case, you may not listen carefully enough to perceive the value of what is being said to you. *Yet it's the alternative points of view that have the potential to give you the greatest help.*

Those among us who are most aware progress along our paths not only with one hand reaching behind to help another, but also with one hand reaching out in front to receive help from another. That help may well come in the form of feedback and messages from your loved one. Your relationship will benefit immensely when you listen carefully to feedback from your partner and study it thoroughly, looking for ways to make use of it. In addition, by listening carefully you honor your partner and, as an extra benefit, win their respect. Your partner will respect and love you all the more for appreciating and being open to hearing what they have to say.

THE POWER OF FREE AND OPEN COMMUNICATION

*We're never so vulnerable than when we trust
someone—but, paradoxically, if we cannot
trust, neither can we find love or joy.*

~ WALTER ANDERSON (1944–)

One way to begin to create Safe Space in your relationship is to set some ground rules with your partner that will ensure that you both can freely and openly communicate thoughts and feelings to each other without criticism, anger, or fear of reprisal. Here are some steps you can take to begin that process.

~ Tell your loved one that you want to create a Safe Space for the two of you and eliminate the element of fear from your relationship so you can both be free to grow, learn, and love.

~ Explain that although it may take some practice,
   you are committed to allowing your partner to
   express fears, concerns, and feelings without you
   criticizing or cutting them off.

~ Get several pieces of paper and write "Safe Space"
   on each one. Put them where you will see them
   regularly: on your bathroom mirror, the sun visor
   of your car, in your wallet with your money or
   driver's license, on the table where you eat, and
   where you work. These notes are a reminder to
   you to keep this concept uppermost in your mind
   when you are interacting with your partner. The
   concept of Safe Space is also valuable to keep in
   mind whenever you interact with anyone.

~ The next time you are tempted to get upset or
   judge your partner for something they did or did
   not do, remind yourself of your commitment
   to provide Safe Space. You can even say aloud:
   "This is a good situation to practice creating
   Safe Space. I'm going to stop and listen now
   without blaming or judging. Please tell me what
   happened and how you are feeling right now."

~ Be patient with each other. Creating Safe Space takes practice—and you will have plenty of circumstances to practice on. The more you succeed, the more grateful you will be for the safe haven you have created and the more grateful your partner will be for sharing life with someone as gifted as you.

LAW 5

Successful Relationships
Require Light from the Past

The past is not a package one can lay away.

~ EMILY DICKINSON (1830–1886)

One of the main requirements for a successful relationship is that you and your partner must know and understand each other in the light of your past experiences. Past relationships have created impressions and behavior patterns that carry over into your current relationship, affecting it in many ways. That includes relationships with parents and friends as well as with other people who have shaped you and your partner, particularly love relationships—the good as well as the bad. Because each of you has had different experiences, you will each react differently to the ever-unfolding events of your relationship. Understanding why others react to events the way that they do is critical to being able to cope with their reactions and to helping them move beyond the pain that may be under the surface.

LAW 5

SUCCESSFUL RELATIONSHIPS
REQUIRE LIGHT FROM THE PAST

SUCCESSFUL, FULFILLING RELATIONSHIPS REQUIRE light from the past. Here is an example of how understanding the past can make all the difference in the course of a relationship. Cory and Tiffany lived happily together for three years except that every Christmas, Thanksgiving, New Year's Eve, Fourth of July, and all other vacation times were full of dissension. Tiffany started fights on those occasions for no obvious reason, destroying the harmony of the holiday. Cory walked on eggshells to avoid conflicts at holiday times, but no amount of caution could save the day from disaster.

Tiffany was by far the stronger of the two personalities. She was an aggressive, outgoing sales agent for an insurance company, while Cory was a quiet, unassertive computer programmer. Cory felt helpless and didn't know how he could remedy the situation. He asked Tiffany if she would go for coun-seling, but the suggestion only made her angry.

After getting some advice from a psychologist, Cory decided to talk with Tiffany about the holidays she had shared with her parents. To create the safe atmosphere for Tiffany to talk about her own family holidays, he started the conversation by reminiscing with Tiffany about his own holidays spent with his parents. After hearing that, Tiffany commented that the holiday times she had spent with her mother and stepfather were filled with dissension and anger. Tif-fany's mother and father had gone through a messy divorce when Tiffany was four years old, and her mother remarried a year later. Her mother and step-father moved several states away from her father, and Tiffany rarely saw her father after that. When Cory asked why holidays with her mother and stepfather were so upsetting, Tiffany refused to talk about it and became distant.

Cory wisely did not press the issue, but he knew he was on the right track. A few days later he began to talk once more about the times he had spent with his parents during holidays. After a while, Tiffany again offered the comment that the time she had spent with her parents at holidays was a disaster. Cory only said, "Oh?" suggestively and she finally told him her tale.

How the Past Shapes the Present

Tiffany's stepfather was a retired army man who saw himself as a tough guy, a hard taskmaster. Unfortunately, he also had a sadistic nature. Immediately after he married Tiffany's mother, he began to mentally dominate five-year-old Tiffany. His favorite ploy to get Tiffany to do what he wanted was to create the illusion that he had a wonderful surprise in store for her.

He would say, for example, "Wait until you see what I bought you for Christmas. You're going to love it!" He would make that statement four or five months before Christmas. Then the next time he wanted Tiffany to do something that she didn't want to do, he would say, "If you don't do it, I won't give you your Christmas present." He would constantly use the threat of not giving her the present right up until Christmas morning, when he would cause a nasty argument. As a result, there would be no present, no matter how good Tiffany had been. Her stepfather destroyed every Christmas day and blamed it each time on Tiffany.

Similarly, her stepfather would promise a wonderful vacation. He would talk for weeks about the vacation, all its wonders, and the fun they would have. Then, when he wanted Tiffany to obey him, he would threaten her with the loss of the vacation. "If you don't do what I tell you to do," he would say, "I won't take you on the vacation I told you about." He would keep that up until the day of the vacation. Then, the morning they were to leave, he would cause an argument that would result in him canceling the vacation, always blaming it on Tiffany.

The same scenario unfolded not only on Christmas but on every Thanksgiving, Fourth of July, Halloween, Easter, Labor Day and Memorial Day weekend, and all vacations. This torturous behavior kept up until Tiffany was about ten, when she started to rebel. She wouldn't wait for her stepfather to ruin the holiday; she would do it herself, and quickly. In this way, she protected herself from hurt and disappointment. When her stepdad would promise a holiday, Tiffany would wait for that holiday to come around and then create an uproar that would ruin the day. Knowing she was going to do that saved her from suffering the disappointment she would have ordinarily felt. That was the conditioning that she was bringing into her relationship with Cory.

Intentional Compassion

Cory told the psychologist about Tiffany's experience with her stepdad, and they created a plan to cure Tiffany's problem. Christmas, always a prime time for arguments, was just a few weeks away. A few days before the holiday, Cory took Tiffany out to dinner. He asked if he could bring up a touchy subject. He said that he knew it was touchy but that it was important to both of them. Tiffany agreed. He told Tiffany that he used to lie all the time and that it had ruined all the relationships he had before theirs. He told her that the last girlfriend he had before he married Tiffany had told him that he would never be able to have a lasting relationship with anyone as long as he couldn't be trusted.

He described to Tiffany how he had gone to see a psychologist shortly after the breakup and how the psychologist had helped him work his way through his early life. With this help, Cory had come to realize that his mother had lied to his father all the time and that he, Cory, was doing the same thing in his relationships. Once he realized that, he began to see that he was the one spoiling his relationships. He vowed never to do that again, and that was one of the main reasons he and Tiffany had such a strong relationship.

Cory told Tiffany that the reason he was sharing this with her was because she, too, had relationship patterns that were a reflection of her childhood experiences. As a child, she had learned to create problems for her family during holidays to protect herself, and that had carried over to their marriage.

Step by step, Cory took Tiffany through some of their ruined holidays and told her that he would never hurt her in any way and that she no longer needed to protect herself in that way. Tiffany cried at the table, and Cory went around to her, put his arms around her, and told her how sorry he was that she had to go through that as a child. If she would trust him this Christmas, he said, they would go slowly through the day, being very careful with each other.

The holiday was a success, a loving success, and so were the holidays that followed. By intentionally being patient and compassionate, Cory created a Safe Space for Tiffany to open up and then let go of the unhealthy patterns that she no longer needed. Without shedding light from the past on Tiffany's horrid experiences with her stepfather, Cory and Tiffany may have suffered through upset holidays for many years or lost their relationship entirely.

Successful Relationships Require Light from the Past

The Power of Sharing Your Life Stories

*Those who cannot remember the past
are condemned to repeat it.*

~ George Santayana (1863–1952)

All of us have gone through painful experiences that have shaped our reactions to our current relationship partners. To have the beautiful relationship you want, you and your partner must share your life stories with each other, holding nothing back. That sharing includes any past experiences of brutality, traumas, rape, incest, and emotional or mental torture of any kind that either of you has experienced as well as the wonderful memories you each cherish. It will help your relationship greatly if you can set aside some time every week to go over with each other one of the items listed below.

~ Talk about the experiences you've each had with others that made you feel abused, damaged, or hurt.

~ Talk about the experiences you've each had that made you feel special or gave you joy.

~ Talk about things your parents said or did that made you feel special or happy.

~ Talk about things your partner's parents said or did that made your partner feel special or happy.

~ Talk about anything that will give your partner insight into who you really are.

~ Talk about anything that will give you insight into who your partner really is.

~ Talk about hopes you've carried for a long time, even those you've given up on.

~ Talk about hopes your partner has carried for a long time, even those your partner has given up on.

~ Talk about your fantasies, your daydreams, your aspirations, no matter how unrealistic or seemingly impossible.

~ Talk about your partner's fantasies, daydreams, and aspirations, no matter how unrealistic or seemingly impossible.

~ Talk about what makes you feel good or special.

~ Talk about what makes your partner feel good or special.

Let the light from the past illumine your relationship today so that you will know how to treat one another in the present to bring about the loving and lasting relationship each of you desires.

LAW 6

THE UNIVERSE IS PERFECT AND IS ALWAYS WORKING TO BENEFIT YOU

The world ... is not imperfect, or on a slow
path towards perfection: no, it is perfect in every
moment. ... Everything has to be as it is, everything
only requires my consent, only my willingness,
my loving agreement, to be good for me.

~ HERMAN HESSE (1877–1962)

The Universe is perfect. That is its permanent condition. It never deviates from that condition. It goes from perfect to perfect to perfect in an unbroken stream of perfection. If you want to know if something is perfect, there are two tests: *Does it exist?* If it exists, it is perfect. *Has it happened?* If it happened, it is perfect. *In the Universal sense, everything that is, was, or ever will be is perfect. The best possible event is the only event that can occur.* The law that the Universe is perfect and is always working to benefit you, standing all by itself like that with no explanation, may not help you much. But once you understand the concept, it will be one of the most liberating concepts you'll ever learn. If you can live by this one concept, you will come to know true happiness and live a stress-free life. You will be almost impossible *not* to love because acting in harmony with that law will enable you to create the environment of Safe Space in which your perfect relationship can grow and flourish.

LAW 6

THE UNIVERSE IS PERFECT AND IS ALWAYS WORKING TO BENEFIT YOU

THE CONCEPT THAT OUR UNIVERSE IS PERFECT IS THE most important concept in my business, in my marriage, and in my life. I use it constantly in everything I do; it is the basis for my entire thought pattern. It governs my response to events and my interaction with people, and it keeps me peaceful and happy. I sum up my philosophy in one sentence: "I am a perfect being in a perfect Universe where everything that happens benefits me."

Reading that, you might think that my life has been miraculously exempt from suffering and pain. Not so. I, too, have experienced the shocks and traumas, the nastiness and childhood tragedies, the broken bones and operations, the abandonment, the embarrassment, the cruelty, the rape, the shame, the ridicule, the beatings, the loss of happiness, the deceit, the trickery, the betrayal, the loneliness, and all the thousand and one events that we are all heir to. The difference between us, if there is one, is that over the years I have learned to draw a different conclusion about them.

What "is" simply "is." As for time, you can't reverse it and cause an event to undo itself. All you can do, without exception, is to react to it by liking it or disliking it—by labeling it "good" or "bad," "lucky" or "unlucky." The events that have caused your feelings are beyond your power to alter, even a little bit. Once the egg has been crushed underfoot, it cannot be put back together again.

EVERYTHING THAT HAPPENS BENEFITS YOU

Remember the little poem about Humpty Dumpty, the egg who sat perched on a high wall: "Humpty Dumpty sat on a wall, Humpty Dumpty had a great fall. All the king's horses and all the king's men couldn't put Humpty together again." Even if Humpty could be put together again, and perfectly, the event would still have occurred. You cannot roll time backward and put Humpty back on the wall, never to have fallen.

That event cannot be undone. What you *can* change are your feelings about what happened.

Suppose Humpty had been a great friend of yours. Suppose you were going to miss him terribly. Suppose Humpty had been taking care of you and now he is gone. You have two choices. One, you can lament his passing every moment, saddening yourself with your thoughts, remembering all the good things he did for you, becoming more despondent as the days go by, until one day you decide you cannot live without Humpty in your life and you kill yourself.

The second scenario is that you wake in the morning, seeing the wonderful sunshine, the fresh smell of flowers outside, the dew on the grass, and you go for a run, feeling exhilarated by all of nature. You think about Humpty and remember all the good things he did for you and feel a rush of gratitude for the wonderful Universe that brought Humpty into your life for all those happy years.

As you think about your life with Humpty, you may also realize that you had, in actuality, become dependent on Humpty, waiting on him to do certain things for you. Although you miss him, you are now free to launch out on your own and spread your wings. You don't have to live under that great wall any longer, in the shadow of it, waiting on Humpty. You decide to move to the seashore and fulfill your lifelong dream of becoming a beachcomber, or you decide to get trained in a new occupation, one that Humpty never wanted you to get involved in. You do that, and soon you are grateful for Humpty's fall, watching your life unfold in all its wonder as you step out of your own shell. Humpty went on to the next stage in life's journey and you went on to yours; and one day you will follow in Humpty's footsteps as your days on this planet come to an end.

Eternity is made of an endless series of "nows." Isn't it always "now"? Fill your "nows" with happy thoughts and grateful feelings and you will come to know the great truth of existence: *you are a perfect being in a perfect Universe where everything that happens benefits you.*

Taking Control of Your Thoughts and Feelings

For you to really understand the concept that everything that happens benefits you, it will be helpful for you to learn how I arrived at my conclusion and began to change how I thought and felt about the events unfolding in my life. The beginning of my illumination took place in the sixth grade. That year I was raped.

I was filled with humiliation and shame, hatred and rage. My self-image was destroyed. I never again saw the person who had violated me; he moved away shortly after the incident, leaving me with a ruined life. Day in and day out, I was tormented with thoughts of killing him in every way imaginable, slowly and torturously. Those thoughts took control of my life during all my waking hours. The years passed and I still writhed inwardly in agony, never free of the specter of the violation, of what I believed to be the destruction of my manhood, my self-image.

One day, when I was fourteen, I was sitting under a tree by myself doing what I always did—visualizing the torture of that person—when suddenly I received the most wonderful Universal gift. I realized that I was inflicting myself with continuous, acute mental pain and anguish, even though the perpetrator was gone and the event had been over for years. I was doing it to myself!

That day, that instant, I stopped destroying myself. An enormous weight lifted off me. I came out of my misery like a ray of light breaking through the clouds on a dark, cold day. Suddenly, I was free. I laughed. I stood up and shouted "Yes!" followed by "What a jerk I've been! What an idiot!"

For the first time in my life, I had taken control of my thoughts. My brain, however, had been so traumatized and my habit so entrenched that my brain would still conjure up the mayhem I had been imagining for that person. As I battled the thoughts away, refusing to let my brain torture me any longer, the agitating thoughts became fewer and fewer. Finally, I succeeded in eliminating them.

During the years that followed, when something happened that hurt me, took something from me, shamed me, or caused me to feel mental pain, I would ask myself if I was the one causing myself the continuing pain. The answer was always yes. And then I would do my best to stop torturing myself. I did not always win that war because my imagination was powerful and my programming was fully in place, as is yours, and I often found it difficult to control what I was thinking, especially if someone had done something to hurt me and I wanted to hurt them back. It was as if my brain was in charge, not me, and I was forced to watch and feel what my brain was running as a film inside my head. During those times I would still suffer, but at least I was aware that I was doing it to myself. As the years passed, I grew more proficient at ending my suffering quickly.

Occasionally, I realized that something that had happened to me that was seemingly bad in fact turned out to be a great benefit. I began to look for other incidents in my life that had initially seemed bad but turned out to be for my benefit. What I came to realize, when I looked closely, was that *all* events, no matter how bad they seemed at the time, were in reality beneficial to me in some way. That's when the major breakthrough came; I realized I had to be grateful for the rape, for the enormous, wonderful, liberating gift I received as a result of it. That incident, terrible though it was, put me on the path for all that was to follow in my life, including the writing of this book.

The Unfolding of "Perfect"

I mentioned earlier that after I had moved across the country to break away from Bea's influence, I came across the ancient Chinese book of wisdom called the I Ching. When writing came to China in 3000 BC, the I Ching was the first thing to be recorded. Before that, it had been passed along in the oral tradition for thousands of years. The I Ching is one of the world's oldest-known branches of wisdom. I studied it not only because of its wisdom and the fact that it contained many Universal laws, but also because within it I discovered my moral code—what the ancient Chinese sages called "the way of the superior person." The term "superior person" does not mean one who puts on airs and struts around, but one who lives a virtuous life.

As I grew in my understanding of Universal laws, I came to see that Universal law governs everything. Once I understood that, I was able to perceive and understand a great many other aspects of the world in which we live. For instance, I learned that all the laws of the Universe are in favor of the continuation of the Universe, a point I touched on in Law 1. How do we know that to be true? Because the Universe continues. Since the Universe has been around in its current form for over 13 billion years, there can be little doubt about the perfection of its construction.

For our Universe to continue to exist, it can only permit the best possible events, perfect events, to occur at any moment in time. If it were otherwise, the Universe would be in danger of its own destruction because one imperfect event could lead to two, to three, to four, and so on, eventually leading to its destruction. The continuation of the Universe depends on the law that the best possible event is the only event that can happen.

In the Universal sense, *everything is perfect. That includes you.* You may only have one arm, but you are a perfect one-armed human being.

Carrying the thought further that the Universe is constructed so that it can continue to exist, it can be said that at all times the Universe benefits itself to the maximum amount possible. Since you are an integral, inseparable part of the Universe, the same thing applies to you: *everything that happens to you benefits you and in the maximum amount possible.* Even if an incident hurt you, shamed you, or took something from you, that event will always work to your complete benefit since the Universe will not let anything bad happen to itself, and you are "itself."

As the decades have moved on, I have continued to live with this philosophy and it has borne itself out through every circumstance of my life, even when what I believe has been put to the fire, sometimes on a daily basis.

Are You Open to the Benefits?

One of the bits of wisdom I learned along the way in life is that as long as you are angry or upset over an event, whether in your relationship or any other part of your life, you will be unable to perceive its benefits, and you may wear yourself out with unnecessary resistance. The event was for your complete benefit from the moment it happened. Again, an event is simply an event; the way you respond to the event is what determines its final outcome in your life. Once an event has taken place, since you cannot alter the past, all that is left to you is your response.

Because the events of your life are for your complete benefit from the very outset, why not respond as though that were true? If you do, you will then immediately experience good feelings about the event, and by acting in accord with your feelings, you will help to bring about that end and not waste endless hours, days, even months or years lamenting something that was for your total benefit from the beginning.

Suppose, for example, that you are feeling really good and are having a fine day when someone drives his car over your bicycle. It's a law of the Universe that every action we take produces a result. So if you react to the broken bicycle, or any event, as though you are the victim of bad luck, you are, in effect, signaling the Universe to respond to you as if you really were a victim. You will perceive the Universe's reaction as more bad luck, but, in actuality, you are causing that response *by your initial reaction*.

On the other hand, if you say, "That's perfect!" and mean it, you will be responding to the incident as though it were a good thing for you. What happens then? Because the Universe is forced to respond to you as you are being at every moment, when you respond positively you bring out its more pleasant aspects, its positive potential, which you then get to experience.

To understand in more detail how this works, let's play out the broken-bike scenario in an exaggerated way. First, imagine that when you see the car running over your bike you run out of your house, drag the driver out of the car, and have a fight. The police come and you're taken to jail, where you are sexually molested. You kill the person who molested you and you get life imprisonment. That's one totally exaggerated option. It's ridiculous, I know, but it makes a point.

Here's another, more enlightened option. You walk over to the driver's side of the car that just ran over your bike. The driver is waiting apprehensively for your reaction. You smile and say, "That was just right, don't worry." Your unexpected reaction produces a rush of gratitude from the driver. You introduce yourself and the grateful driver offers to pay for the damaged bike. Your response is, "That's fine, I'll accept the payment, but let's take a moment and see if this event occurred because we needed to meet."

As a result, you and the driver become life-long friends, you marry his sister, you have a wonderful family, and you spend many years together in great pleasure. Additionally, suppose that, unbeknownst to you, the bolt that held the front tire on your bike was loose, and the next time you would have ridden the bike you would have had a serious accident going down a steep hill. The bike getting run over would actually have saved your life.

Act according to the belief that every event unfolds only to benefit you completely and you'll cause every event to continue itself along those lines. *You are completely in charge of the aftereffects of the event.* As William Shakespeare wrote, "There is nothing either good or bad, but thinking makes it so."

Here's another example of how that works. About twenty years ago, my son Pax and his friend Aaron were at home with me when the telephone rang. I answered it and found out it was a caller who had dialed the wrong number. The caller apologized and was about to hang up the phone when I said, "Wait! Maybe this isn't a wrong number; maybe we're supposed to talk. It could be a lucky coincidence." We spoke for a few minutes, telling each other about ourselves, but then said goodbye, not finding any connection between us, although we had a good laugh about it.

Seventeen years or so later, Aaron, now about twenty-seven, received a "wrong number" phone call. He remembered my call many years earlier and he said to the caller, "Wait! Maybe we're supposed to be talking to each other." After talking for a few minutes with the girl who had called, he found out that she was a cheerleader for the Miami Dolphins football team. He had always had a long-held dream of dating a cheerleader. The next day, Aaron, who lived in Los Angeles, was on a plane to Florida. He stayed with her for a week or so and they came back to California and moved in together.

In all areas of your life, staying open to the benefits of unexpected events will free you to open up to the opportunity that has entered your life. In addition, it will fill every day with happy expectation.

Start with Small Things

The questions I usually hear in response to the concept that the Universe is perfect are "If the Universe is perfect, what about Hitler and the holocaust?" "What about 9/11?" "What about the tsunami that killed over two hundred thousand people in Thailand?" "What about infant death or cancer?" "Why do I have pain?" "Why did my dad die when I was only seven?" "Why did my cat get run over?" "Why did my lover leave me when I gave the best years of my life to that relationship?" "If this is such a perfect Universe, why is there so much turmoil, strife, and suffering?"

Those are tough questions. Looking at events in the world and in our own lives, it seems as if there could be no such thing as a perfect Universe. We have all experienced what seems like bad luck, misfortune, even tragedy. We have been lied to, cheated, had our hearts broken, and been betrayed by loved ones. In the face of that, how could this be a perfect Universe?

The short answer is that in some way, even if we don't immediately see it, those events are part of the perfection of the unfolding Universe and it is only our perception that is incomplete. And you do not want to get caught up in thinking "If my perception is flawed and I'm part of the Universe, that means the Universe is flawed as well." The answer to that is that your seemingly flawed perception is perfect for you at that moment in time; in actuality, your perception is not truly flawed but is in the process of evolving.

How do you get to the point of believing in a perfect Universe? You start with little things: the lost wallet, the broken watch, the missed bus or plane, the stubbed toe, the broken vase, the stolen bike, the lost dog or cat, the dented fender, the cut finger, the lie you've been told. Even in the face of what you would normally think of as rotten luck, you must be patient, reacting as though it were the best luck possible, knowing and trusting that you will eventually find out why it was the best luck possible.

Your reward for following that belief is an increasing, conscious control over all situations and a far more pleasurable now, heightened by your vision of a bright and happy future as well as memories of a pleasurable past that saw you following your belief with sureness.

How does this new way of thinking, feeling, and acting play itself out within our relationships? Remember the example I gave with Law 4 about your partner or spouse getting into an accident with the car? Rather than seeing it as a cause for anger, hollering, sarcasm, or meting out penalties, respond as if it were a perfect event. Say "That's perfect, honey. You'll probably meet your new best friend when you take the car to the shop to have it repaired or maybe the mechanics at the repair shop will find something else that really needs to be fixed to make the car safe." Likewise, if your spouse drops the heirloom that has been in the family for six generations, you'll be in step with unfolding events and set the right tone by responding with "That's perfect, dear. I was tired of caring for that vase anyway."

What you show your partner or spouse by reacting like that is not only that they can trust you to hold a Safe Space for them no matter what happens, but also that you *value your relationship and the love you share more than any loss or disturbance.* Just as importantly, those incidents no longer have the power to ruin your day, your month, your year, your relationship, or your life.

REFRAMING THE PAST

An important part of embracing the law that everything that happens is for your benefit is learning to adjust how you see and feel about past events that you may still be lamenting. I was in New York being interviewed on television, radio, and in newspapers for my book *The Alcoholism and Addiction Cure* and a reporter came to interview me who had been drinking heavily. He reeked of alcohol. We talked for a couple of hours, and when the interview was over I asked him why he drank. He said it was because he was the victim of a missed opportunity early in his life. I asked him to tell me about it.

He said that he had had an opportunity as a young man to go to Harvard University and didn't take it. He explained that now he worked only part time as a reporter and that his regular job was driving a food-delivery truck six days a week starting at three in the morning, a job he was not very fond of. I asked him if he was married and he told me that he was married and had six children, that he loved his family very much, and that they were the joy of his life, the best thing that had ever happened to him.

I asked him what he had done instead of going to Harvard and he said he had attended another college, a small one without much of a reputation.

"Did anything significant happen to you there?" I asked.

"Yes," he said, "That's where I met my wife."

"What!" I exclaimed. "You're drinking because you missed going to Harvard University and instead met your wife with whom you had six wonderful children?" I saw that all his years of disappointment had come from his lamenting an event that was, in reality, a huge benefit to him.

After he thought about it a minute, he said, "You know, you're quite right." A few months later, I received a letter from his sister telling me that her brother had quit drinking and was a changed man. He had freed himself from his addiction to alcohol by realizing that life was not conspiring against him but had been working to his benefit all along.

Are you feeling stuck because you are clinging to the belief that the course of a relationship or a decision you made or an event that took place in the past ruined the rest of your life? Many people still carry around hurts or regrets from past relationships. Some people even lament a divorce that took place years ago, even though today they are happily married to someone else. Others feel that the best part of their lives is behind them because someone they loved left them. If any of these scenarios is the case for you, you can change that right now.

All of us have had our hearts broken. When it happened, we were distraught and unhappy, but then somebody else came along and we got into another relationship. If we had known when the first relationship broke up that that would be the case, we would probably have treated the breakup much differently.

If you knew that an ending in your life was opening the way for an even better relationship with someone else, would you be unhappy? No. You would say, "Thank you for getting me ready for the next person!" Or even "Oh, we're through? Okay, please move your things out quickly; I have someone new coming along fairly soon."

If you knew at the moment you got served with divorce papers that something twice as good was coming, would you be upset? No. You'd say, "Ah, this is my graduation certificate so I can move on!" What happened in your past wasn't an unfortunate mistake; it was for your ultimate benefit.

Having that attitude from the start, even when you can't see what's coming next, will open the way for that new relationship or that new condition to come to you much more quickly. That's how it works all the time with all the situations in our lives.

Let me tell you a little story about how I taught my son Pax that lesson. He was about three-and-a-half years old. He had gotten a new bicycle a few months before and he loved it. One day, we rode to the beach, chained up his bike, and went for a swim. When we returned, the bike had been stolen. He began to cry. I asked him how he felt about the loss of his bike.

"Bad!" he shouted.

I asked him if it hurt and he said, "Yes!"

"Where does it hurt?"

"Here," he said, pointing to his chest. Then I asked him how he felt about the person who had stolen his bike.

"I hate him!"

"And what would you do to him if you found him?" I asked.

"I'd hit him with my bat! I'd make him give me back my bike."

"Didn't you tell me that you were out with Mommy last week and saw another bike you liked better than the one that was stolen?"

He thought for a moment and said he remembered that.

"Well," I said, "let's go see if that bike is still in the store."

We drove to the store and bought the bike. I took Pax and the bike back to the same place where his bike had been stolen. I asked him again how he felt about his bike being stolen.

"Bad!" he said, but without the same depth of emotion.

"And what would you do to the person who stole your bike if we found him?"

"I'd hit him with my bat!"

I'm sure you see what's coming. I pointed out to Pax that if his bike hadn't been stolen, he wouldn't have the new bike. We spent about half an hour on the topic until I had made the point clear enough for his three-and-a-half-year-old mind to kind of get the point. I worked on that with him on and off for the next few months, and then for a year or two after that when similar incidents would occur. Today, those lessons serve Pax well. Of course, he'd use it against me every so often when he had done something I didn't want him to do. He would say, "It's perfect, though—right, dad? The Universe couldn't continue if I hadn't done that, right?" I would point out that he was right in that those incidents were definitely giving him the lessons he needed—and he would have to keep on learning those lessons as long as he kept up that same behavior.

LETTING GO OF REGRETS

If you can't get into the mode of thinking that the events that unfold in your life are for your ultimate benefit, you will continue to carry old baggage around with you. You will drag it along with you wherever you go. And what are you doing by continuing to drag those regrets behind you? You are preventing yourself from being happy today, because every time you think about those regrets, you say to yourself, "What bad luck..." You're destroying that moment by allowing past events to tyrannize you. But if you can adopt the philosophy that everything that happens is perfect, all the people you think you lost and all those heartbreaks suddenly become just right. In reality, it cannot be otherwise because you are a part of the Universe, and the Universe takes care of itself perfectly.

Look, I know this is a difficult concept because of all that's gone before in your life, but the effort you put into understanding this will be repaid a thousandfold when you are successful in responding as though the events in life are always working in your favor.

When seemingly negative situations come into your life, whether it's heartbreak or an unexpected turn of events that seems "bad," the real question is not "Why me?" but "I wonder how this will benefit me?" What you may have been accustomed to doing up to this point is grieving. You lament, you feel bad. But that's a choice—a choice you can change. You can choose to adopt a new outlook—one that's bright, cheerful, and fully expectant of something wonderful that the event is part of.

When something happens that seems unlucky or bad, I treat it as if it's great. I don't lose my good mood. I don't get down in the dumps over it. And as the days pass, sure enough, I find out that it *was* perfect for me. Maybe what seemed like an obstacle prevented me from making a bad business decision or allowed me to put my time and attention into something much more important or brought me into contact with someone I needed to meet. That's the world I live in every minute, every day.

I invite you to live in that world also, to start seeing that things have happened to you and will happen to you for a reason—so that you can be benefited in the maximum amount possible. In fact, there is no other event that could have occurred that would have benefited you in any greater amount.

The Power Points in Your Life

One of the ways we benefit from events, which isn't always obvious until later, is that the situations and relationships we find ourselves in always provide us with exactly what we need to move forward and make progress. Think of it like this: When the Universe was created, everything was used up. There was no box full of left-over, unused galaxies, earths, mountains, waterfalls, or stars. Everything was used up and it was in the exact right place. It still is, and that includes you.

The Universal intelligence is vast beyond anything we can conceive of; it is not stupid. When Pax was thirteen, he said to me: "The most difficult thing to do has already been done—the creation of the Universe. After that, everything, in comparison, is easy." Can we create a flower, a stone, a banana, a fish? If we cannot do that, how can we think of the creation of the Universe and not feel complete and total awe and reverence?

The Universe was created at exactly the right moment to allow for the creation of our planet and our solar system. Earth cooled at exactly the right moment to allow for the evolution of life forms. We were born, each of us, at exactly the right moment to allow us to arrive at this moment in time. Everything that happens is always at exactly the right time. You cannot be out of place in the Universe. Wherever you are, that's where you're supposed to be, doing whatever it is that you are doing. And whether or not you are happy depends on your state of mind as you are doing it.

We are always at the perfect place at the perfect time to experience the perfect event for our perfect understanding, which is for our perfect growth. Knowing that can help you stay perfectly sane and perfectly happy under even the most perfectly trying of times. After all, we are here to perfect ourselves as human beings, as spiritual creatures.

You may have heard that we are not human beings here on earth to have a spiritual experience, but we are spiritual beings here on earth having a human experience. At times, the way the Universe helps you perfect yourself is to bring seemingly unpleasant events into your life so that by the very overcoming of those obstacles, you will gain strength, wisdom, and the information you need from those events.

At the end of your life, when you look back on it, you will see that your wisdom and your strength didn't come from the average, ho hum, nothing-happening kind of day. Those were rest periods in between growth opportunities. Your wisdom and strength came from the power points in your life: the turmoil, the abandonment, the rape, the loss of loved ones or the loss of love, the loss of opportunity, the betrayal, the humiliation, the seemingly costly mistakes you made and the so-called accidents.

The Universe does not bring a circumstance into your life if you no longer need it. When you are in the first grade, you learn that one plus one equals two. When you are in high school, you no longer get that lesson because you already know it. It's the same with the conditions in your life. When you have gotten the information you need from a circumstance or situation in your life, it will pass away. If you have not gotten the information, the situation or circumstance will either remain in your life or will repeat itself.

Earlier in the book I talked about my friend who said that he had had the worst luck choosing women and complained that the last nine girlfriends he chose all turned out to be bitches. Do you remember that after he discovered that he was the one causing his relationship problems that he found his true love and they have remained together and have a wonderful family? Well, that's how it works. If you have any situation in your relationship you're unhappy with, be open to the information you are receiving so you can understand *why* that condition is part of your relationship.

If you find yourself in relationship after relationship that has the same unhappy pattern or the same issues that lead to a disappointing breakup, see that as a cosmic tap on the shoulder, a wake-up call, a gift of information to you from your Universe so you can correct your destructive behavior and save your relationship or prepare for a new one. The tap on the shoulder is meant to get you to stop, look objectively at your relationships as if they were pictures laid out on a table, and see what you need to change. It is meant to show you what adjustment you need to make in your thoughts, your expectations, and your behavior so that you can become the kind of person who will attract and maintain the kind of relationship you want and, most importantly, receive the love you desire.

Who You Are with Is Not a Mistake

The interactions you have with your loved ones are among the most important ways you are meant to learn and grow. The person you're in a relationship with is not a mistake, a cosmic error. Nor is it happenstance, a chance encounter. The person you're in a relationship with is the right person for you at this moment in your life. The relationship you are in is the one you are *supposed* to be in so you can get out of it whatever you are supposed to get out of it: information, wisdom, strength, and self-improvement. That does not mean you are supposed to stay in that relationship if it is hurtful or unsatisfactory, but you are supposed to be in it for the time you are in it— and by learning about the Laws of Love, you may indeed create the most wonderful, loving relationship that lasts a lifetime.

So please, don't misconstrue what I'm saying here to mean that you should accept an intolerable or abusive situation in your relationship. Sometimes the piece of information you are meant to receive is the warning that it's time to move on before you are harmed. Learning from the situations of your life does not mean you should be a doormat or a punching bag. If you are in a dangerous situation, physically or emotionally, seek support and take steps to protect yourself.

Throughout the process of learning to accept that the Universe is perfect and is always working to benefit you, you'll benefit greatly if you can be patient with yourself. Learn to see that within our perfect Universe the challenges in your relationships, the ones that push you beyond your comfort zone, are for your ultimate benefit.

Again, I know it may be hard to believe that because of what's gone before in your life, but if you can open your mind to this concept, if you can allow just a little crack of light to sift in and say to yourself that this might be possible, even though it seems impossible, you will be opening yourself to all the good things that the Universe has been providing you and has in store for you. And no matter how good you can imagine it, the Universe can do it better. No matter how great your dream is, the Universe can dream it better.

THE POWER OF
LOOKING FOR THE BENEFIT

We either make ourselves miserable, or we make
ourselves strong. The amount of work is the same.

~ CARLOS CASTAÑEDA (1925–1998)

One of the main reasons so few people are truly
happy is because of faulty perception and lack of
knowledge, not bad luck. When you treat an event
as if it were bad luck, you give it the power to be
bad. When you treat it as good luck, you create a
chain of events that brings about positive results.

Another way to look at it is like this: When
you are angry over an event, it's like wearing blind-
ers. Your attention is focused on the object of your
anger while the Universe continues to unfold in
all its wondrousness. You are still stuck in the moment when the event took place, anchored there

by your anger, missing out on what could be the most important moments of your life happening right now.

Here are a few simple steps you can take to begin to see the events in your life as perfect and as always being for your absolute benefit.

~ First, call to mind a situation from the past that at the time seemed "bad" but later turned out to benefit you. For instance, you may have had your heart broken but later found a new partner and experienced a wonderful love relationship. The second relationship would not have happened without the first relationship ending. In addition, the heartbreak was part of the experience you needed to have in order to be able to comprehend what you are learning here today. As you think about the past event that turned into a blessing for you, allow yourself to feel gratitude that this first event paved the way for you to experience something wonderful.

~ Now bring to mind a current situation in your relationship that has hurt you, angered you, burdened you, or that you have labeled as "bad" or "rotten luck." Instead of thinking of yourself as a victim, tell yourself: *This situation is perfect. I know that it is for my ultimate benefit. There is some vital information or lesson I need to receive from this experience.* That can be a tough assignment, but you can do it. Pretend if you have to, but assume that the situation is *entirely constructed for your benefit* and open yourself to seeing what that benefit is.

~ Whenever you are tempted to feel like a victim, make this simple shift in awareness once again and remind yourself: *the Universe is causing every event that occurs in my life so that I can be benefited in the maximum amount possible.*

The following words from the poem "Desiderata," written in 1927 by Max Ehrmann, are a beautiful reminder of that truth:

You are a child of the universe,
no less than the trees and the stars;
you have a right to be here.
And whether or not it is clear to you,
no doubt the universe is unfolding as it should.

LAW 7

YOUR RELATIONSHIP WILL
PROVIDE WHAT YOU NEED

*There are secret forces at work
leading together those who belong together.*

~I CHING (CA. 3000 BC)

You have probably heard that like attracts like and opposites repel. Well, that's only partly true. What you attract is what you need; what you repel is what you don't need. There are forces constantly at work bringing together those who belong together. That is part of ancient wisdom that has been handed down for thousands of years. That means you need have no concern about meeting the exact right person for your perfect relationship. You will attract a partner who has what you need for you to continue refining yourself into as good a human being as is possible.

LAW 7

Your Relationship Will
Provide What You Need

It is the Universe that brings people into your life. The seeming chance encounter is your destiny unfolding. Here's a short story to illustrate that. My wife, Lyn Hamaguchi Prentiss, who is of pure Japanese ancestry, was eighteen years old when she went into a building to get a book from a college classmate. As she walked through the hallway, she noticed a light green drafting table that looked exactly like the one her father worked on at home. She went over to it and saw a grey-and-yellow book titled *I Ching* lying on it. Lyn opened the book and read some of it. It is a very complex book, having been written thousands of years ago. She put it down, thinking to herself that she would like to spend some time getting to know it later in her life.

Twenty-six years later, Lyn was living on the island of Kauai, the northernmost of the Hawaiian

Islands, and had gone to visit her girlfriend Takako, who is also Japanese. She was browsing through Takako's library when she saw a book with *I Ching* in the title. Excited to find something on that subject after so many years, she picked up the book and brought it to Takako, who said, "My friend wrote that book."

The book Lyn was holding was one of the seven books I have written, under my Chinese pen name Wu Wei, about Chinese philosophy and the I Ching and about the Universe and how it works. The next time I was on Kauai, Takako introduced me to Lyn.

That is the "coincidental" way Lyn and I met. The Universe prepared Lyn twenty-six years earlier for that meeting. It may be important to state here that twenty-six years in Universal time is less than a trillionth of a beat of a hummingbird's wing. That's how the Universe works. You may say that it was merely coincidence, but that's just a word we use to describe the amazing and miraculous way the Universe brings together those who belong together and other "coincidental" cosmic happenings.

You can be in a room with hundreds of people and the one you gravitate to will be the one the Universe has chosen for you to become acquainted with. Later, if you have a relationship with that person, you'll tell friends how you met and how amazed you both were that in that crowded room you found each other. If you ask the next ten couples you see how they met, each one will most likely have a story to tell about the "coincidence" that brought them together. That's how it works. Relationships are arranged by Universal choice.

In a sense, then, all relationships are prearranged. You may be a person who wants to marry someone who is wealthy. That may be your major criteria, your highest guideline. But if you eventually marry someone wealthy, it will be because the Universe provided you with a wealthy person who possesses the attributes that will enable you to grow in all the necessary ways. That person's wealth and your desire for wealth were how the Universe attracted you to that person.

You will be drawn to someone by looks, personality, accomplishments, character and manners (or lack of them), and all the other characteristics that go into making up a human being. But know that what is wrapped up in all those aspects is "what you need."

THE PURPOSE BEHIND THE PARTNERSHIP

It is time to cast aside any doubts you may have as to the awareness of the Universe and its purposefulness in bringing you together with those you are meant to be with. The Universe brings you together with others for a purpose, and that purpose is so you can learn from each other and perfect yourselves as human beings. There will be good times and probably passionate times; if there weren't, you wouldn't stay together. But there will also be friction, disagreements, different ideas, different values, and different modes of expression. There is a design to that. What bothers you most about your relationship partner is almost certain to be the very issue you need to work on.

If you are the kind of person who is impatient or easily becomes angry, you may very well find yourself in a relationship with someone who will provide you with plenty of practice in developing patience and compassion. If you are a worrywart or are overanalytical, your partner may be someone who is intuitive and spontaneous. If you can't draw good boundaries, your partner may be someone who doesn't respect boundaries very well and there-

fore forces you to develop that much-needed quality. And, of course, you may be there to teach your
partner how to respect boundaries.

To improve your relationship, take a look at
the areas of dissatisfaction and see what information your partner and the circumstance are bringing
you. Another way of saying that is that whatever is
in your life right now is what you need right now.
Whatever level you are at, what you need at that
level will come to you naturally. The Universe will
bring it to you in a manner that seems entirely coincidental. And when you are ready to go to the next
step in your evolution, the mate you need is waiting
for you (or is already in your life but unrecognized
by you), having been hand-picked by the Universe.
That is the Universal Law of Attraction.

Of course, as I mentioned in the last chapter,
and it bears repeating, I am not saying that you should
tolerate a toxic relationship that is truly unhealthy for
you if you happen to be in one right now. There are
any number of reasons you may find yourself in such a
relationship, including that you have to learn to value
yourself more so you can end dangerous liaisons and
learn to focus on what you deserve.

Who Is Attracted to Us

A key but often forgotten ingredient in relationship dynamics is that we attract people to ourselves who match our current level of development. We tend to think about the kind of partner we want in our lives, but an equally important factor is who we attract by being the kind of person *we are*. Ralph Waldo Emerson expressed this when he wrote: "See again the perfection of the Law as it applies itself to the affections. . . . As we are, so we associate."

I've seen this concept in action many times, but one in particular stands out to me. In 1985 and 1986, I led workshops in Los Angeles for people who didn't have the life they wanted and who were willing to come and work with me for a month to gain control of their out-of-control lives. We always sat in a circle, and when the first workshop began, I would go around the room asking each person what it was that they wanted.

The answers were varied: get a home of my own, obtain financial independence, find my soul mate, get ahead at work, take over the company I work for, move out of my parents' home, learn to date, find peace, and many other things that most of us long for. Had you been in that workshop, you would have said that one of your goals was to learn how to create or attract the relationship you've always dreamed of.

One man in the group who was searching for his ideal mate reported that a few months before he came to my workshop, he had taken a workshop to learn how to find his ideal mate but it hadn't worked. This man was about fifty-five years old, about twenty-five or thirty-five pounds overweight, hadn't shaved for a couple days, wasn't well dressed, and had driven up in an old Chevy in obviously poor condition.

When I asked him what he had learned in that workshop, he said that the workshop leader had told everyone to make a list of the attributes each of them wanted in his or her ideal mate and to carry the list with them at all times. I asked if he had his list with him, and when he said he did, I asked him if he would share what was on his list. He pulled out a two-page, single-spaced, typewritten list and read it to us.

Among the items he had listed were that he wanted a partner who was beautiful, physically fit, and about five feet six inches tall with a very slender figure, large breasts, and long, wavy dark brown hair. He wanted her to have a friendly disposition and a great desire to please him. He also wanted her to be talented in massage, an excellent cook, a good piano player, gifted as a lover, and a good skier as well as financially well off because he had never been able to find success in business and was currently working as a day laborer. His list was truly amazing.

I looked at this man and I said to him, "Where's your list?"

"What do you mean?" he said. "This is it."

"No," I said, "where's your list for *yourself*? The one that matches hers. Are you a good cook, a good masseur? Can you play a musical instrument, do you consider yourself an exceptionally handsome man, or do you have any of the other qualities that would match the list you wrote for your dream partner?"

"Well," he replied, "I can ski."

"If the woman you described walked in here right now," I said, "and saw the man who had called her forth, she would probably think someone was playing a huge joke on her. You need a list for yourself that matches the qualities of the woman you described in your list. I suggest that you make a list for yourself, and when you have achieved the attributes that are the equal of the ones you want in your ideal mate, she will appear."

Life doesn't work the way this man thought. Here's the way it actually works: you must be worthy of your mate. I'm not saying that you have to possess the exact same characteristics as the partner you would like to have. In fact, we often attract to ourselves those who have qualities we don't have but who balance us out. If you are not a raving beauty or a ruggedly handsome man, that doesn't mean you cannot attract a raving beauty or a ruggedly handsome man. But you must have other good qualities and common bonds of interest that will attract that kind of person into your life—and keep them there.

ATTRACTION IS NOT LOVE

Most of us are unaware of why we are attracted to certain people. As I wrote earlier, your concept of your ideal mate was formed as you experienced your own relationships and observed those of others. You've probably seen others who are in relationships you wish you had, and you've probably seen others in relationships you're glad you don't have. You've also learned ideas about the "ideal" mate from family or from what you've read or seen in the media. Those ideas are largely in our subconscious and we are unaware that we hold those ideas.

When you see someone and feel an attraction, it's due to their image resembling the image you hold in your subconscious mind. As you get to know someone's character better, you will either be further attracted or repelled due to the experiences you have had in your lifetime and the lessons you have learned.

The problem with relying only on our attractions is that *relationships usually end when the attraction ends.* As the sixteenth-century Renaissance thinker Montaigne once observed, "I see no marriages which sooner fail than those contracted on account of beauty and amorous desire." Attraction may be what draws us to another to create a relationship, but it is not what keeps us together. Attraction is not love. Attraction blooms in the beginning of a relationship because of physical attraction or sexual attraction or because a certain need is being fulfilled, but those impulses will all wear off, some sooner, some later. Even if you're a person who is fun to be around, that in itself will not be enough to hold the two of you together.

Sometimes people come together based on a common interest that they share at one point in their lives. What happens, though, after that purpose has been achieved or when they are no longer able to pursue that common purpose? What happens if one or the other partner isn't interested in that goal any longer?

Say, for example, you and your mate were attracted to each other primarily because you shared an all-consuming passion for rock climbing or scuba diving or some project or another. Then after you married you lost interest in rock climbing or scuba diving, or the project ended and you no longer engaged in that activity with your mate. If that is the only bond you share, the two of you may move apart emotionally and the relationship may end.

So if you form a relationship based on a common purpose and expect it to endure based only on that, you may be disappointed, because after the purpose has been achieved, unless some new purpose arises to create a bond, the relationship will most likely end. People who lived thousands of years ago knew this essential truth, which was taught in the I Ching: "A relationship formed on the basis of a common interest lasts only so long as the common interest lasts." To have a quality, long-term relationship, *you have to be able to move beyond the attractions that first brought you together and share long-term, relationship-sustaining goals.*

At the beginning of each relationship and throughout that relationship, you must build common interests with your partner. Be involved in their life. Don't be a bystander. If those long-lasting bonds are lacking in your relationship, find some shared pursuits quickly. Taking an interest in your partner's personal life is one of the best ways to find something that will take you both beyond the initial attraction. For example, discover how you can assist your partner in a business venture, a project, a hobby, or a sport. Perhaps you can become friends with your mate's family or friends or help your mate fulfill a long-held dream or desire. To uncover what that area of interest might be, talk to your partner about their hopes, dreams, aspirations, and plans. See how you can fit into them.

THE POWER OF
LEARNING FROM YOUR PARTNER

*There are no mistakes. The events we bring upon
ourselves, no matter how unpleasant, are necessary
in order to learn what we need to learn.*

~ RICHARD BACH (1936–)

In every relationship, there will be good times and
not-so-good times. There will be rewards and problems, joys and unhappiness. In the midst of all that,
you are polishing each other. You will learn from
each other, change each other, and bring about the
Universal plan for each other. The learning goes on
as long as you are together.

Here is a statement to ponder and consider
making your own: "*I am in my mate's life and my
mate is in my life for the express purpose of perfecting
ourselves as human beings and to have fun doing it.*"

Sometimes this process may not seem like
fun, but remember that the challenging times are

sometimes the most productive times. Always be looking at what's going on in your relationship as a learning time.

Take a few minutes now to think about your current relationship—the person you are with, how you treat each other, and how you feel about your relationship. Then think about how your relationship fills your need to learn and grow by answering these questions:

~ What is my partner teaching me (through words, actions, or example) that I need to learn in order to grow at this stage in my life?

~ How am I bringing my partner what they most need to learn in order to grow?

When you use what happens within your relationship to self-reflect and adjust your behavior, you are not only learning and growing as a person but you are also becoming capable of building a better relationship.

IF YOU WOULD BE LOVED,
LOVE YOURSELF

One must learn to love oneself...with a wholesome and healthy love.... It is of all the arts the finest, subtlest, last, and most patient.

~ Friedrich Nietzsche (1844–1900)

If you do not treat yourself with love and respect, as someone worthy of being loved and respected, how can you expect others to treat you that way? Loving yourself has to do with the image you hold in your mind of who you believe yourself to be—your self-image. Bring to mind any situation within a relationship—how you act on a first date, how you express or don't express your needs to your partner, how you react or overreact to a perceived criticism—and you can be sure that your self-image has something to do with the outcome you experience. If you haven't taken the time to create a wonderful self-image for yourself, you have most likely had less, been less, and done less than was possible for you. You can learn to love yourself, which, in turn, will cause your partner to love you. You can improve your self-image at any moment, including this one.

LAW 8

IF YOU WOULD BE LOVED, LOVE YOURSELF

WHEN I TALK ABOUT LOVING YOURSELF, I AM NOT talking about becoming like Narcissus, the extremely handsome but haughty lad in Greek mythology who falls so in love with his own reflection in a pool that he cannot leave it and thus wastes away and dies. The love I'm talking about has nothing to do with being so caught up with your own accomplishments or success that you become egotistical, or being vain about successful family members, acquaintances, or famous friends. And it has nothing to do with physical beauty or social status. Rather, the love I'm talking about is the regard you hold for your personal attributes of good character.

If you are not an admirer of yourself, it's because your self-image is tarnished. You know your inmost secrets. If what you know of yourself causes you to think little of yourself, it's because of things you've done or haven't done. Perhaps you know yourself to be unkind, thoughtless, a liar, untrustworthy, not a good friend, a betrayer, or a mean or selfish person. Perhaps you have impure thoughts or desires that are unworthy of a person of high ideals. Perhaps you think you're not a great beauty, not a good conversationalist, not a fast thinker. Perhaps you haven't been able to get ahead in life and feel unsuccessful. The implications of who you believe yourself to be are far-reaching.

"WHO YOU THINK YOU ARE"

When you walk into a room and meet someone for the first time, it is "Who You Think You Are" who walks into the room and "Who You Think You Are" who speaks and acts. If you do not regard yourself highly, you will project that to the person you are meeting. A diminished self-image will cause you to slouch, to avoid meeting others, to avoid looking others in the eye, to be unassertive, and to be indecisive. On the other hand, a healthy self-image will cause you to carry yourself well, to speak confidently, to be outgoing, and to portray dignity.

If you have difficulty making friends, it's because "Who You Think You Are" is manifesting itself. If you have difficulty getting ahead at work, it's because those surrounding you are reacting to "Who You Think You Are." If you have difficulty finding someone to have a relationship with or you can't seem to create a loving relationship where you feel valued, it's most likely because your self-image is damaged in some way and is manifesting itself in such a way as to thwart your goal.

As a simple example, let's say that one morning you wake up late and are in a great hurry to get to an appointment with a friend you haven't seen in a while. You don't have time to go through your morning routine of making yourself presentable, but throw on what you were wearing yesterday, wrinkled and smudged. Hair not brushed, you rush out the door to get to your meeting, knowing you're going to be late anyway. When you reach the appointed meeting place, your friend has not arrived yet. You sit down at a table to wait, and there, at the next table, sits the person of your dreams.

That person turns to look at you. You know you look terrible, your mismatched clothes hastily thrown on and your hair not brushed, and you are certainly not in the best state of mind. "Oh my God!" you think to yourself. "Here I am, sitting next to the person who could be my ideal partner, and I look like a train wreck." You fidget, you squirm, and you'd like to be anywhere else except sitting where you are, looking as you do. Needless to say, your self-image at that moment will not be conducive to the start of a great conversation and you will most likely make a poor first impression.

Contrast that to this scenario. You know that you have an appointment in the morning to meet your friend. So you get a good night's sleep, wake early, and pick out a nice outfit, one that suits you to a tee. You groom yourself immaculately and set out for your meeting. You arrive a little early, and when you take a seat you find yourself sitting next to your dream mate. You can imagine the difference between the two states of mind—you in your dishevelment and despair, and you dressed to the nines and feeling really good about yourself.

In essence, how you feel about yourself will manifest in many ways—actually, in every way. It will be reflected in the way you shake hands with someone, the way you meet their gaze, the way you walk, your mannerisms, your speech, the way you carry yourself, how you enter a room full of people, and what you think of yourself when you look in a mirror. It will also manifest itself when you meet the person of your dreams. There is help for a ruined self-image, and later in this chapter I will offer a powerful technique to dramatically improve your self-image, but for now it's enough to know that you must change your down feelings about yourself to really good feelings about yourself if you hope to be loveable.

THE ROOTS OF YOUR SELF-IMAGE

I wrote earlier about how the beliefs you hold about life, meaning your personal philosophy, affect your relationships. It's not just the beliefs you have about how the world works that fashion your life and relationships. The beliefs you have about yourself, about what you are capable of, and about what you deserve are also important.

The moment your brain became functional, you began to build that image of who and what you believed yourself to be. All the events of your life have helped to create the image of "Who You Think You Are." Perhaps a parent told you from the time you were very young, "You're wonderful, and I love you." Those words will remain in your memory, supplying you with that information no matter what else happens to you. Each time someone is critical of you, the words of your parent will still be there: "You're wonderful, and I love you." It is a fortunate child who receives that kind of positive image-building.

On the other hand, you may have had experiences that reinforced the opposite belief. Perhaps when you were a child, you were given a new toy that you broke shortly after receiving it, and the parent who gave you the gift exclaimed, "You're so clumsy!" That criticism may have hurt you. Maybe you thought about it a lot. Perhaps the following week you bumped into a table, knocked over a lamp, and it broke. Perhaps someone saw the incident and said, "Watch what you're doing, clumsy!"

Afterwards, when you dropped something or hurt yourself, you may have thought to yourself, "I'm so clumsy." Although many years have passed and you've forgotten the original incidents, those words are there feeding you from a subconscious level, saying, "I'm clumsy."

Your parents or those primarily responsible for your upbringing were not the only ones who contributed to your self-image. Children, siblings, friends, and other adults participated in your image-building. Imagine for a moment that when you were in the second grade, you were attracted to the child with the soft brown eyes. Imagine that you went over to the child and very timidly said, "Would you like to eat your lunch with me?" And the child replied, "What! Eat my lunch with a creep like you? I'd rather eat my lunch with a toad!" You crept back to your desk, hoping you were the only one who had heard the remark. The embarrassment and hurt impressed itself upon your mind. You began to form an image of yourself as seen through the eyes of the person who made the remark.

It probably took a long time for you to make such an attempt again. Imagine the next time you tried to do the same thing, perhaps years later, and with a different person. You may have said something like, "Ah, well, um, I, ah, was wondering if you would like to, ah, maybe, um, well, you know, eat your lunch with me?" Perhaps the person laughed at you and said jeeringly, "Duh! No thanks!" The image of yourself that you had formed from the first experience influenced the way you acted the second time, which, in turn, helped to create the second harsh response, reinforcing and solidifying your negative self-image.

After two such harsh image-forming events, it is doubtful that you would make another attempt for many years. By that time, even if those two events had faded from your memory, the image they created would still feed you from a subconscious level, still influence the way you act, and still be a strong part of "Who You Think You Are."

You can probably imagine how experiences like that affect your relationships. I'm sure you have some stories of our own—times you were embarrassed, times you were made fun of, times when you thought you didn't measure up. What's imperative to remember is that the essence of who you are is not what other people say you are, or even who you think you are at this moment. In reality, who you are is an indestructible child of a golden Universe. *Simply being part of the Universe is the greatest honor anyone can have. You have been chosen—chosen to exist, chosen to be here at this moment in time when you can have the greatest relationship possible.* The Universe is magnificent and so are you. Work with that. Get to feel it, believe it, know it in your inmost heart.

The idea that people are less than perfect has given rise to the saying "Well, I'm only human," meaning we are lowly humans who naturally make mistakes. Only human? What a huge put-down! How about wonderfully human, fabulously human, stupendously human, miraculously human, fantastically human, phenomenally human, *gloriously* human? Did you learn from your mistakes? Of course you did. But most of the time, people emphasize your "mistake" rather than the lesson you got out of it.

What you usually heard when you were growing up was "You're wrong," as though there was something wrong with *you*. The people in your life probably didn't say, "That was a mistake, but you are a perfect being learning to use your body and brain, which is done by practicing. And in practicing, you'll make what seem to be mistakes, and you may *seem* to fail, but you're always a perfect being, evolving along your own path to enlightenment." But that is the truth.

RESHAPING HOW YOU THINK ABOUT YOURSELF

While the beliefs you harbor about yourself can be deeply entrenched, causing disappointment, sorrow, and even addiction, they are not irreversible. One of our clients at Passages Addiction Cure Center, Simone, a thirty-year-old woman, believed that she was unattractive. She hung her head much of the time, slouched, and held her shoulders forward to hide her well-developed breasts. She grew her hair long and let it hang down so it hid a good portion of her face, and she said she had a difficult time mingling with people.

Her parents believed Simone was unattractive, and they were the ones primarily responsible for creating her poor self-image. Her mother was fond of saying, "Simone, you are going to have to learn to please people with your personality because you'll never get along on your looks." When Simone was nine years old, her dad told her, "Simone, don't feel bad because you're not as pretty as the other girls in your class. Daddy still loves you." Crippling remarks!

When her parents called Passages in Malibu, I received the telephone call. They told me that their daughter's major problem was that she was unattractive and she knew it. I was surprised, then, when I met Simone, for I thought she was quite beautiful. After two weeks at Passages, her therapists came to me and said they knew what the problem was, but they weren't making any headway with Simone and they asked if I would see what I could do. I agreed to talk with her.

"I can't help it if I'm unattractive," she lamented during my first meeting with her.

"Simone, you are one of the most beautiful girls I have ever seen," I replied.

"Please don't make fun of me," she said.

"Simone, look at me," I urged. She hesitantly looked at me, but then quickly looked away.

"Simone," I said, "please look into my eyes and don't look away." It took a few moments, but she finally did it.

"Simone, I swear to you that you are one of the most beautiful girls I have ever seen."

I asked her to stand in front of a mirror with me. She was reluctant, but I insisted. As we stood together in front of the mirror, I asked her to look at herself. She said she didn't want to, and I begged her to do it just that one time, for me. I asked her to stand straight, and then I pulled her hair back from her face and piled it on top of her head. I asked her to smile at herself. The difference was so amazing that even she could see it.

Simone's month of treatment at Passages was a tough one, and very embarrassing for her at the start, but she followed the advice of our therapists, kept her hair swept back from her face, learned about makeup, held a broomstick behind her shoulders to straighten her posture, and dressed in a way that added to her already great beauty. When she left Passages, she looked and felt like the radiant woman she truly was, as if she had been reborn, which, in fact, she had been.

When her parents came to pick her up I was standing nearby and saw her mother's mouth actually hang open. She put her hand to her cheek and said, "Oh, my God." She couldn't believe what she was seeing. Her daughter, who she thought was so unattractive, was standing in front of her as beautiful as anyone could possibly want to be. During Simone's final week in treatment, we mostly worked on getting her to forgive her parents for the injustice she had suffered at their hands. After her treatment was over, Simone moved to Malibu and became a successful model. If you could see the difference between the woman who walked into Passages and the woman who walked out of Passages a month later, you would understand how crucial it is to have a good self-image.

CREATING YOURSELF AS YOU WANT TO BE

On the following pages is a simple exercise that can help you create a wonderful self-image, which will ultimately help you create the relationship you desire. The exercise comes from another book I have written called *Be Who You Want, Have What You Want.* Try it now as you read this. You can return to this exercise as often as you wish or need to.

In this exercise, you will journey to what is called the alpha level, where you will use your imagination to create an image of yourself that will overwrite the image you currently hold in your sub-conscious mind of "Who You Think You Are." Your new image is the one that is "who you want to be." The first part of the title of the book this meditation comes from is *Be Who You Want*. This exercise plays a major part in bringing that about. Once that is achieved, the second part of the title, *Have What You Want,* will naturally come about.

Without being aware of it, you have struggled most of your life to live as your perfect self while you were fighting to overcome the negative effects of the "assumed" image that was impressed on your mind by parents, teachers, friends, and even yourself as you began to believe the negative things you were told about yourself. You are going to end that struggle by creating a new image that will match your perfect image.

The alpha level is a state of mind that is very re-laxed. You go through the alpha level just before you fall sleep and just as you are waking up. When you are in that drifting state of almost awake, that's the alpha level. At that level, you are very open to suggestion.

When you mentally go to the alpha level, every-thing can be just the way you want it to be and imagine it to be. Once there, you will meet your subconscious perfect image and experience that image with your conscious mind. When your conscious mind experiences your subconscious perfect image, it will be powerfully influenced by the experience. It begins to act as your perfect image would act if it was the only image you had of who you are. Acting as your perfect image, you will naturally bring about new results—results different from the ones your old, flawed image produced. You will see yourself the way you were meant to be, as you already exist on the "perfect image" subconscious level.

That means that you will see all of yourself as perfect—your physical self, your career self, your social self, your student self, and all the other selves that make up you. You will saturate the part of your mind that is your everyday consciousness with subconscious images of your perfect being. You are going to overwrite the flawed image you hold of yourself with a wonderful, bright new image that is the real you.

The results of that will be that you will feel immensely better about yourself, you will act from the deep level of your subconscious perfect image and, of course, you will produce results consistent with your perfect image. This is one of the powerfully effective ways in which you will become who you want. Once you have achieved that, can you imagine that your perfect self will bring you *what* you want as well? Of course it will!

As you experience the journey to the alpha level as you read the following pages, allow yourself the luxury of letting go. Allow yourself to flow with the words. Read slowly, and as the words unfold, pause often and let your imagination have full reign. At first, this takes a high degree of concentration because thoughts of the day will intrude into your thinking process. Consciously push those thoughts aside and keep your attention fixed on what you are doing.

It helps to have soft music, without vocals, quietly playing in the background. Flutes are a good choice. If you elect to have music playing, be sure that the recording will last at least as long as your journey, perhaps twenty minutes.

At the alpha level, you will see things in a certain way. Whatever way you see them is correct. If, for instance, you hear that you are to imagine golden stairs, whatever kind of stairs and in whatever shape you imagine them is correct. They can be spiral or straight, round or square. They can rise quickly or slowly. Whatever you see is correct for you. If you hear that you are to imagine a pond, the pond can be as wide as a street or as wide as a football field. Whatever you see is correct for you.

You may think you are conjuring up your perfect image with your imagination. That is not so. You are actually bringing your perfect image forth from the Source of All-That-Is, where it already exists. The same is true for the fields, pond, rocks, flowers, waterfall, and other parts of your place of ideal relaxation that you are going to call forth from the Source. I capitalize Source to help you keep in mind that your Source is the conscious, totally aware Universe. You are not alone; the Universe is aware of your quest. It is aware of what you are now doing. It will assist you.

If you're going to have soft music playing, this is the time to start it. Turn off the phones and TV and guard against interruptions. Give yourself up to this exercise. Allow your mind to roam freely in this perfect world of your imagination. Don't hold back.

Meditation on the Perfect You

To begin this liberating journey, find a comfortable chair, and relax. Slowly expel all the air from your lungs and hold it out for a moment.

Now, ever so slowly, inhale. Slowly, slowly fill your lungs to capacity, and now, hold your breath, perhaps for three or four seconds. Slowly exhale, mentally repeating the word *relax* three times. When your lungs are empty of air again, wait quietly for a moment.

Next, slowly inhale, filling your lungs to capacity. Now hold it and then slowly exhale, mentally repeating the word *relax* three times.

Experience what a good feeling it is to be so relaxed. Feel your eyelids relax. Move your head from side to side and feel your neck muscles relax. Allow this feeling to float slowly downward, relaxing your whole body.

As I name each part of your body, momentarily tense the muscles in that area and then relax them. Now feel your face muscles relax...your shoulders...your chest...your back...your arms...your wrists...your hands and fingers...your waist...your hips and thighs...your knees...the calves of your legs...your ankles...your feet and toes.

Now slowly expel all the air from your lungs and hold it out, perhaps for three or four seconds. Now slowly, slowly inhale, filling your lungs to capacity, and hold it, perhaps for three or four seconds, then slowly exhale repeating the word *relax* three times.

Read slowly. Now that you have slowed your breathing, you're ready to experience a deeper, more relaxed level of mind. Mentally count backwards from ten to one—one number for each inward breath, and one number for each outward breath. With each descending number, feel yourself becoming more and more relaxed as your mental cycles begin to slow and you drift to the level of mind just before sleep. As you count, allow yourself to drift slowly down to the level just before sleep.

Ten—nine—eight—one breath for each number, drifting slowly downward, drifting, drifting. Seven—six—five—like a feather floating softly down, down to the level just before sleep. Four— three—down and down. Two—one.

You are now at a deeper, more relaxed level of mind, and you are calmer and more peaceful. Use this deep level of mind to go to an even deeper, more relaxed level of mind. Slowly expel all the air from your lungs and hold it out for a moment. Now slowly, slowly inhale, filling your lungs with air, and hold it for a moment. Now slowly exhale, going deeper and deeper to the level of mind just above sleep.

This is the level where all things are exactly as you wish them to be. This is the level of power where you are always in complete control.

Now imagine rolling meadows, covered with lush green grass. In your mind's eye, see beautiful flowers of many different colors all around. The sun is shining gently. A soft breeze is blowing, moving the grass gently. There are big, inviting rocks scattered around. Birds fly about and sing. Butterflies float gently on the breeze. What a perfect spot this is. Experience what it feels like to be in this meadow.

In the center of the meadow is a pond. Trees grow near its edge. Some of their branches hang gracefully down and touch the water.

Walk over to the pond and look down into the crystal-clear water. See the tiny, colorful fish swim by—friendly fish. See the reeds growing by the side of the pond and a small island in the center.

On the other side of the pond is a waterfall about ten feet high, a magical waterfall, whose waters come from the Source of all things. See the water as it plunges over the edge and into the pond. See the sunlight glinting on the water and the rainbow that's created as the spray drifts on the wind. Walk over to this waterfall and feel the spray. The temperature is just right. Now let your clothing disappear and step under the gentle waterfall. It is exactly the right temperature. Ah...how good that feels.

Mentally put your hands over your head and turn around. Feel the water as it cascades down over your hands and arms, your head and shoulders, your chest and back—refreshing you, cleansing you, washing away all that you wish to be free of. Feel these magical waters as they wash away your tiredness. See the tiredness as dust being washed away, leaving you strong and refreshed, vital and alive.

Feel the magical water wash away all feelings of resentment and frustration. Allow any feelings you have of resentment and frustration to dissolve and float away from you, released by the waterfall. Allow all guilt and anxiety, all feelings of sinfulness and depression to wash away. See them as dust, washed away by the powerful waters, dissolving, and leaving you clean, whole, pure, innocent, virtuous, and free.

These magical waters heal you of all manner of ailments. Give yourself up to the healing power of this magical waterfall. Feel the healing nature of the water as it washes over you. You can breathe in this water. Breathe in this water now. Feel the water as it courses through your body, purifying every cell, every bone, every organ, causing them to sparkle and glow with health and vitality. Feel the remarkable water cascading over and through your whole body, exhilarating you, filling you with its power. Feel the waterfall wash away everything you wish to have washed away, leaving you pure and free. Now take a deep breath through your nose and let it out quickly through your mouth in a "whoosh" sound. And now do it again.

Step out from under the waterfall and stand beside the pond. Feel the sun gently warming you, cleansing you, purifying you. Feel its rays shining through you, filling you with its radiance, causing you to glow and shimmer. Feel the wind softly drying you—penetrating through you, healing you, causing you to feel light and free. Now cause yourself to be clothed in a white robe, soft, light, and luxurious.

Mentally create a seat for yourself. It can be of any material you like—wood, cloth, even air. For you, it's the most comfortable place in all the world. Settle yourself into the seat now, and relax. Feel how absolutely comfortable that is—how perfect. See the blue sky, the occasional white puffy cloud, the birds flying by. Everything here is exactly as you wish it to be. Here you are in complete control. This is your perfect place of ideal relaxation and peace. It is more uniquely your own than anything else on earth. You have called this place forth from the Source of all that exists and it is truly yours. Here you get to decide the way everything is. Here you are completely in charge.

Now call forth the image of your perfect being by seeing yourself exactly as you would like to be. See your perfect image standing, facing you, about five feet away, clothed in a white robe, the same as yours. See everything you could ever want to be. See how natural you look. Look at your hair, see what color it is. See your skin and notice the texture of it. Have your perfect image raise its hands over its head and turn about. Look closely at the back of your image. Have your image continue turning until it faces you again. How graceful. How full of poise.

Get up from your seat and walk over to your perfect image. Look into the eyes of your perfect image. See how clear they are. Smile at your perfect image and see your perfect image smiling back at you. Your perfect image knows everything there is to know about you—and loves you completely.

Hold out your right arms toward each other and clasp wrists. Feel the energy and power leaving your perfect image and passing to you. Feel yourself glowing. See your perfect image glowing.

Release wrists and see your perfect image turning around and facing away from you. Walk closer to your image and step right into it, merging with it.

Now, as your perfect image, put your hands over your head and turn around. See how wonderful that feels. How graceful. Dance about a little. How light and strong! Walk over to your most comfortable seat and rest a moment as your perfect image. What a good feeling. How relaxed, how much in control you are. This is the real you.

Repeat the following sentences in a whisper:

From this moment forward, I am in control of every situation. I will always know the exact right words to speak. I will always know the exact right action to take, and this is so. I will now obtain vibrant good health. I will have the possessions I want, I now have the power and wisdom to bring this about, and this is so. I will have peace and harmony in my life. I will have love in abundance, and this is so. I now claim all these things for my own from this time forward.

Take a few minutes now to create for yourself in your imagination your most perfect relationship. Close your eyes and see it in great detail. See yourself interacting with your partner. Experience what it feels like to be totally loved and experience what it feels like to totally love your partner. Feel the love. See yourself being cherished, cared for, nurtured, pampered, trusted, and being able to completely trust your partner. Feel the to-die-for trust. See it stretching out to the end of your days. Enjoy your perfect relationship now that you have finally experienced it. Know that whatever beneficial thing you have envisioned is even now on its way to you, and this is so.

Now that you have envisioned what you want, it is time to ascend to your new life. Across from the pond are ten golden stairs that lead up to a new everyday consciousness. See the sun as it sparkles on the stairs. See how they shine. As your perfect image, walk over to those stairs now.

Shortly, you will ascend these stairs with all the power, love, and peace you have visualized for yourself here in this perfect place of power and ideal relaxation. You will ascend these stairs, leaving behind all the things that were washed away by the waterfall and that dissolved into nothingness. You are free. You are pure. You are whole. You are virtuous. You are powerful. You are a person able to feel love and to accept being loved. Hold that image of yourself powerfully in your mind.

Slowly climb these golden stairs now, one step for each inward breath and one step for each outward breath. One—two—three—four—five. Pause, turn around, and look over this paradise you have created for yourself. See the pond and the trees and the flowers. See the waterfall and the blue sky. There is a magnificent rainbow arching from one side to the other. See how it glows and shimmers. Here in this perfect place, everything is exactly the way you wish it to be.

You may return here anytime you want to. Just by desiring to be here, you will be here instantly. Here you may refresh yourself in the waterfall, washing away fatigue and frustration and anything else you wish to be gone. You may breathe in and drink the healing water and fill yourself with virtue, power, and healing. You may rest in your seat and call forth from the Source the things or events you desire. You can receive ideas and inspiration, and you can create possessions or situations you want for yourself.

In this ideal place, you can have your perfect image appear at any time so that you can once again look lovingly at each other, seeing how you have grown more like your perfect image every time you return. Most important, refresh your mind with images of your perfect relationship. If you find yourself in a bumpy phase in your relationship, go to your perfect place of ideal relaxation and seek guidance. Clear your mind of the problems and see instead the ideal picture you want. Let the solutions come to you.

Now, as your perfect image, continue climbing the stairs to your everyday consciousness, one breath for every step. Six—climb with power and virtue and love. Seven—feel refreshed. Eight—feel very calm and peaceful. Nine—feel more alert. Ten—feel very rested, as if you have slept soundly and well. You are now here, as your perfect image. Your perfect image does not lie, has no bad habits, is all powerful, is completely virtuous, is free to come and go as you choose, is at one with All-That-Is, and loves you completely. Trust it to know what to do in every situation. Trust it to know how to care for you and those in your care. Trust it.

The journey you have just taken is a huge asset in becoming who you want to be and in bringing about what you want to have. When you bathe your conscious mind with the image of your perfect being, your conscious mind becomes saturated with the assets, virtues, and powers of your perfect image.

Soon, as you continue with this exercise, you will begin to act from the level of your perfect image, and consequently you will create results in conformity with your perfect image.

As the weeks pass and you become familiar with your perfect image, you will naturally and effortlessly begin to act as your perfect image. When you're talking to another person, doing a chore, or are engaged in other activities, imagine yourself as your perfect image and allow yourself to be that way. By being "Who You Are," you create your reality, moment by moment. *The Universe always responds to you as you are being at every moment.*

"Who You Think You Are" will change as you follow this program. It is now going through the same process a caterpillar goes through to become a butterfly. Let the process happen and fly. Believe you are the extra-special person you meet in your alpha-level journey, because on that level you *are* that person. By experiencing your perfect image, you will bring that being to the surface of your life and everything will be different for you—far better, far brighter, far easier, far more possible. Drop all aspects of "you" that are apart from your perfect image, aspects like fear, smoking, alcohol, drugs, swearing, weakness, lying, meanness, stinginess, and all limitations that are obstacles to achieving your goals.

The image of "Who You Think You Are" has been around since the day you were born. Your perfect image has been around since the dawn of time. It is one with eternity. It is as bright and as fresh and as powerful as the first brilliant day of the Universe. It is all powerful. It is you.

This journey and meditation is also available on audio so you can just close your eyes and let my voice guide you along the path to restoring your self-image (visit PowerPressPublishing.com to learn more about the audio, called *Meditation on the Perfect You,* or about the book *Be Who You Want, Have What You Want*).

THE POWER OF NURTURING YOURSELF

Love yourself first and everything else falls into line.

~ LUCILLE BALL (1911–1989)

Loving yourself starts with nurturing yourself. Caring for yourself, physically and emotionally, will have far-reaching effects in your life and in the life of your relationship as those around you respond to the way you treat yourself.

Apart from the issue of self-image, one important reason to love yourself is a very practical one. When you love yourself, you will take care of yourself. And when you are in a relationship, what you do to care for and strengthen yourself will in turn nurture and strengthen your partner and your relationship.

As I was working on this book, I asked my wife, Lyn, who is a doctor of Traditional Chinese

Medicine, to share what she thought were the key ingredients to a successful relationship. One of the things she shared with me makes this point beautifully. "Taking care of your physical, mental, and emotional well-being is the same as taking care of your partner. It is the seed of the ability to share happiness," she said. "Working on yourself everyday to bring out the best in yourself is the same as working on the partnership. It represents the building blocks of your partnership—your future."

If you're wondering where to begin loving yourself more, start with the foundation of self-care: your body. Your body, mind, and emotions are interconnected. The state of your mind and your mood affect your physical state. Likewise, the state of your body is a key factor in how you think and feel. To put yourself in a healthy frame of mind—and attract to yourself the healthy, loving thoughts of others—start by making changes in how you treat your body, how you care for yourself.

~ Ask yourself: What one thing can I do this week to nurture and care for my body? Perhaps it's sitting down and eating healthy meals that

energize you rather than weigh you down,
eliminating an unhealthy food or substance from
your diet, or getting more sleep. Identify one
step you will take to make your body feel more
vibrant, and commit to doing it.

~ Add exercise to your schedule. Move. Dance.
Run. Jog. Ride a bike. Jump up and down. Do
calisthenics. Rebound. Jump rope. Swim. Do
push-ups, pull-ups, crunches. Move it! Get out
of breath! If you don't do that every day, you
are cheating yourself of one of the finest, most
productive aspects of life. You can involve your
spouse or partner in this activity with you. And
laugh—a lot.

LAW 9

THE HAPPINESS YOU SEEK CAN
ONLY COME FROM WITHIN YOU

*Each morning when I open my eyes I say to myself:
I, not events, have the power to make me happy
or unhappy today. I can choose which it shall be.
Yesterday is dead, tomorrow hasn't arrived yet. I have
just one day, today, and I'm going to be happy in it.*

~ GROUCHO MARX (1890–1977)

Many people have the idea that if they could just find the perfect partner, they would be able to have the perfect relationship and happiness would forever be theirs. That belief is why you may find yourself jumping from one relationship to the next with the same unsatisfactory results or perpetually focusing on and complaining about some annoying behavior of your spouse or partner. If you think the way to fix your relationship is to fix your partner, it's because you are depending on your relationship for your happiness. The consequences of doing that are huge. When your sense of happiness and the smile on your face depend on what your partner does or does not do, you will either be happy or sad as your relationship rises or falls or as the mood of your partner rises or falls. There is only one thing you can depend on to make you happy: you.

LAW 9

THE HAPPINESS YOU SEEK CAN ONLY COME FROM WITHIN YOU

IF YOU EXAMINE YOUR MOTIVE FOR DOING ANYTHING, even seeking the relationship of your dreams, you will find it's because you believe it will make you happy. That was one of the most important lessons I learned from the participants of the workshops I held years ago. I asked everyone on the first day of each new workshop why it was they had selected the workshop goals they had chosen. The answer was always the same: "It will make me happy." Everyone was seeking happiness. One woman claimed that she didn't want happiness for herself, that she wanted it for her children. Yet when I asked her why she wanted that, the answer was "It will make me happy." That is *everyone's* primary goal on this planet.

I asked one woman who was attending my workshop in the hope of finding her ideal relationship if she would be willing to give up that search if she could be granted absolute happiness for the rest of her life. She said she would give up her search immediately and gladly. I think you'll find that's probably true for you as well. I write that not to deter you from your goal of seeking the ideal relationship but to make you aware that, in actuality, there is another, more primary goal that is more important to you—that of obtaining happiness. That simple change in perspective can make a huge difference in your relationship.

Knowing that happiness is also your mate's goal will make it easier for you to help your mate achieve it, particularly if you communicate your newfound information. For example, how many times has someone made a request or a comment or acted in a certain way and you said to yourself, "What are they thinking?" Well, now you know. Like you, your relationship partner is motivated by what they think will bring them happiness or help them avoid pain. When you understand this and when you put yourself in their place, you'll be able to be more compassionate. You may not agree with what they are saying or doing, but you'll understand that their real goal is happiness, and that will always help you come to a better resolution.

The One Constant: You

While you should take the best possible care of your relationships, remember that you came into this world alone and you will depart from it alone. Rather than burden your relationships with the task of making you happy, make yourself happy by the quality of your own thoughts, by living in harmony with the truths of the Universe, and by living up to your fullest potential day by day. When you have accomplished that goal, not only will you be happy and at peace, but you will also be able to make your partner happy because your partner will be in the company of a happy person.

The truth that only you can make yourself happy or sad is much more empowering than depending on something outside of you to bring you the happiness you seek. It means that you are in control and that you can change your circumstances by making new choices.

Look at it this way—every plan in which you participate, every activity in life, has one constant: you. I don't mean that you are always the same but that you are always part of the plan. All else comes and goes—friends, parents, possessions, conditions, situations, associates, even relationships. Therefore, *real happiness comes from the one component that is always present: you.*

I understand that if your partner is angry a lot or grouchy, it's hard to maintain a happy state of mind. That said, you must do it anyway. There's an ancient saying that "pleasant manners succeed even with irritable people." If you do not allow the irritability of others to affect your own pleasant conduct, you will not only be happier yourself but your pleasant conduct will then influence them. "Your success and happiness lie in you," Helen Keller once said. "Resolve to keep happy, and your joy and you shall form an invincible host against difficulty." Or as the Dalai Lama teaches, "Happiness mainly comes from our own attitude, rather than from external factors. If your own mental attitude is correct, even if you remain in a hostile atmosphere, you feel happy."

Taking personal responsibility for feeling happy about the ever-unfolding events of life does take practice. Because of all the conditioning you have undergone before this, it may be very difficult to make the change. But if you take this truth to heart—that you have the power to choose the way you want to feel—and put it into practice, as the days unfold you will find yourself living an ever-happier life, smiling more and eventually laughing more.

You are the doorway through which life unfolds. Everything you hear, taste, smell, feel, see, or experience in any way is life unfolding through you. If you can keep aware of that and intentionally choose to be a doorway through which happiness can unfold, you will be a joy to be with, a joy to live with, a joy to love.

Each of Us Must Walk Our Own Path

So far I've been talking about this law from your perspective—how you might be putting the responsibility for your happiness on your partner, subconsciously blaming others for how you feel. But the reverse is also true: you should not be responsible for making your partner happy, at least not all the time. You can do so for short periods, but lasting happiness is each person's personal responsibility. You are not supposed to be the puppet master, keeping your puppet smiling and happy with one trick after another.

Sometimes, because of the way we were conditioned, we blame ourselves if our marriage or relationship doesn't work out, even though we have done all we can to make it work. You may even find that you are constantly trying to shape yourself into your partner's image of what his or her perfect mate should be like, look like, and act like. In doing that, perhaps you're denying who you really want to be, who you really are, because you have the mistaken notion that you are responsible for your partner's happiness. At the other end of the spectrum, you may find yourself getting upset or angry with your partner, not realizing that it's because you are rebelling against their expectation that you should make them happy. You can see how this one mistaken concept—that others are responsible for making us happy—can wreak havoc in relationships.

You must walk your own path. Every spider web is different from every other spider web. The face of every person is different from every other face. No leaf is the same as any other leaf. Every snowflake is different from every other snowflake. Everything is different from everything else—the diversification in the Universe is *total*.

Can you not therefore surmise that the path to enlightenment and what you must do to fulfill your reason for being here is different from every other person, and must be different? You are meant to walk your own path, even if it is alongside another with whom you are in a relationship. That means that within your relationship you must still take responsibility for yourself and maintain your individuality. You must still be you.

THE POWER OF
CHOOSING TO BE HAPPY

*My philosophy is that not only are you responsible
for your life, but doing the best at this moment puts
you in the best place for the next moment.*

~ OPRAH WINFREY (1954–)

Learning to live according to the truth that the happiness you seek can only come from within you can be profoundly life-changing. If you find yourself blaming your relationship partner for how you feel, you are, in reality, giving up a huge opportunity to take action yourself and thereby create meaningful change in your life and within your relationship.

Change starts with awareness. Here are some questions you can ask yourself to reflect on your own happiness habits:

~ When I feel upset, out of sorts, depressed, or unfulfilled, do I blame my spouse or partner, friends, family, even my co-workers or boss for making me feel that way rather than looking at how I might need to adjust my own thoughts, feelings, and actions?

~ Do I think that if my partner stopped saying or doing a certain thing, my life would be a lot better?

~ Do I believe that not having a spouse or relationship partner is a major cause of my unhappiness?

If you answered yes to any of those questions, do your best to adjust your thinking so that you take responsibility for how you are feeling—so that you take specific steps to make yourself happy. The way to be happy is to *be* happy.

As a free-thinking, free-willed person, you have the power to choose the way you want to feel. In every instance, if you *choose* to be happy rather than sad or angry or hurt, you will find that at the end of a day, a week, a month, a year, a lifetime, you will have spent a great amount of time being happy.

LAW 10

YOUR RELATIONSHIP WILL
ENDURE WHEN YOU MAKE IT
YOUR PRIMARY PRIORITY

Endurance is the crowning quality.

~James Russell Lowell (1819–1891)

All relationships run the danger that disagreements and misunderstandings will arise that can cause a parting of the ways. In the face of those dangers, if you permit yourself to drift along without keeping in mind the absolute goal of the continuation of your relationship, you may find that your relationship continues or not, as the day may determine. To endure is to continue to the end— to continue in the face of obstacles, pain, fatigue, frustration, opposition, or hardship. Endurance is a state that is not worn down by anything. By committing yourself to the goal of endurance, the goal of permanently maintaining your relationship, you are setting a standard against which you can measure all of your actions and decisions.

LAW 10

Your Relationship Will Endure When You Make It Your Primary Priority

To enjoy a meaningful way of life and produce a long-lasting relationship, you must place the continuation of your relationship above everything else. Say, for example, that your relationship partner has not learned or been taught to feel secure about relationships. And let's say you have a friend you've been exceptionally close to for years. Suppose your partner feels threatened by that friendship and wants you to stop seeing that person. Perhaps your partner is jealous or suspects that an attraction exists between you and your friend or believes that your friend is influencing you improperly. It may be because of any one of hundreds of other reasons, real or imagined. What do you do?

If you are committed to an enduring relationship, the decision is clear: you stop seeing your friend. It does not make a difference whether what your partner feels is based on reality or not. The goal is the survival of your relationship. That means that you give up the relationship with your friend immediately, gladly, willingly, and with good spirits. You do that because you make *all* decisions that affect your relationship on the basis of your relationship continuing and thriving.

Putting Your Relationship First

There will probably arise in your mind many reasons why you should continue seeing your friend. You may think to yourself: "My partner is being unreasonable. I should be allowed to have a friendship outside of our relationship. I am being unduly controlled. Why should I suffer because my mate is jealous and paranoid?" You might even ask yourself: "If I have to stop seeing my friend because my mate is insecure, is the relationship worth it? If I give in to my mate's request to end my relationship with my friend, where will this end? What will be next?" or "That's not a fair request—I have rights too. Why does everything I do have to be done in the light of my decision to protect and preserve the relationship?"

But there is only one real question: "If I continue to see my friend, will my relationship suffer?" If the answer is yes, you go to your friend, explain the situation, and put the relationship with your friend on hold.

All the reasons that will come up in your mind about why your partner's feelings are invalid and unfair must be put aside, because for relationships to endure, that kind of commitment, thoughtfulness, and care is required. Wouldn't you like to have someone care about you in that way?

This is a black-and-white issue, no grey areas at all. You either put your relationship first or risk jeopardizing your relationship. Your failure to acquiesce to your mate's request will find you unhappy and quarreling with each other. The very foundations of your relationship will be shaken and undermined.

When you were growing up, perhaps a parent or guardian powerfully infringed on your rights as a human being. Perhaps you vowed to never let that happen again, and here it is, happening again. Although you may feel as if you are fighting for your rights as an individual, the message to your loved one is that your relationship with your friend or the principle that you are fighting for is more important to you than they are—and that would, in fact, be true. Simply put, if you persist in seeing your friend, you will be violating one of the Laws of Love, and you *will* pay a price for it.

Once your mate is secure in the knowledge that your relationship with him or her is the most important aspect of your life, and when the imagined threat is eliminated, you can then go about *gently* exploring the possibility that the danger your friend poses to your relationship is only in the mind of your mate. Perhaps after your mate sees that there is nothing to fear, you can resume your friendship with your friend by bringing your friend around to meet or spend time with your mate. Perhaps you will all become friends. On the other hand, if you refuse to give up seeing your friend, as a result of natural law you may well lose your relationship.

DECIDING TO PROTECT YOUR RELATIONSHIP

Here's another example, one I touched on with Law 2. Suppose you get a job offer that would mean you have to spend a lot of time away from home, and your spouse objects. What do you do? You pass on the opportunity. Even if taking the job seems essential, you pass on it. If you were to absolutely, ruthlessly adhere to this Law of Love, not even a matter of financial survival would be an excuse to make a decision that threatens your relationship.

Say you decide you want to go back to school so you can develop a skill or talent. It's a big commitment and, as a result, your spouse and perhaps your children may be required to make some changes and adapt to your new schedule, taking more responsibility around the house for a time. What if your spouse flatly refuses to take on the extra responsibility? What do you do? The answer is clear: after exhausting all the possibilities, if a satisfactory resolution is not possible, you must, at least temporarily, give up the idea of returning to school. Again, this is a black-and-white issue. You must decide to either risk or protect your relationship.

A frequent situation that arises in relationships has to do with the family of one or the other of the partners. Family members can ruin a relationship if permitted to do so. Suppose someone or even several members of your family dislike your partner. You

must make every effort to heal the relationship between your family and your partner. Be creative; try
everything you can think of to remedy the situation.
In the end, however, if you are unsuccessful in bringing peace, you will have to severely limit your association with your family or even break it off completely.
It's a difficult decision, but you must always choose
to protect your relationship with the person you love
and have chosen to spend your life with.

In a nutshell, all decisions and actions that will
affect your relationship must be made by answering
this single question: "Will the action I am consider-
ing have a negative impact on my relationship?" If
the answer is yes, don't do it.

The standard is simply this: you must put your
relationship first, ahead of *everything* else. If all the
decisions you make regarding your relationship are
made on the basis of the survival of the relationship,
the Universal Law of Cause and Effect will naturally
cause your relationship to continue. You have a lifetime to build your relationship into the beautiful
creation you envision, but you won't even get the
chance to do that if the relationship doesn't survive
in the first place.

This true story about a famous couple whose names must be kept secret shows the ramifications of making choices that don't put the relationship first. This couple married when the woman was in her early twenties and the man was a bit older. She was sweet, beautiful, and rather naïve. They had a wonderful early marriage and had several children. He was hugely financially successful and they became well known.

As the wife evolved, she decided to capitalize on her fame and started a business, which flourished. Then she started another business and then another until she was running half a dozen and was doing business internationally. At that point, her husband divorced her.

She and I met about ten years after the divorce and she was still heartbroken over the loss of her marriage. Crying, she said she couldn't understand why it fell apart. I told her that the reason was most likely that her husband had married a sweet, tender, innocent young woman who later became an international businesswoman who traveled widely and was heavily involved in business decisions on a daily basis. He already had more money than either of them could spend in a lifetime, and he didn't want a wife like that. The proof of this was that his next wife was a young, tender, naïve person who filled the bill perfectly.

I'm not saying that both partners can't be fulfilled and run successful businesses or each have their own pursuits, or that a husband or wife should remain unfulfilled. What I am saying is that decisions have consequences. In this case, if this woman and her husband had taken the Laws of Love into consideration as the years unfolded, they might have taken a different approach to the issues that arose. The woman could have asked herself—and her husband—if being heavily involved in business was going to impact their marriage. Similarly, if her husband had valued their relationship above everything else, he might have been honest with her about how he felt before they reached a crisis point. If the two of them had taken into consideration what he wanted as well as her desire to express herself in a business career, perhaps they could have found a way to meet both their needs. And if not, then the divorce would not have come as such a surprise and disappointment to this woman.

You can see from all these examples that the decisions you need to make when you become a partner in a relationship are oftentimes different than the decisions you would make when you aren't in a committed relationship.

DEAL BREAKERS

There are, of course, situations that I call deal breakers, which demand a firm approach. Here are a few of them.

Addiction: Suppose your partner uses drugs or alcohol to excess and it is threatening your relationship and your safety too. What do you do? You protect the relationship and insist that the excesses end. The same is true for other addictive behavior—gambling, pornography, sex addictions, excessive TV or Internet use, or any addictive behavior that threatens the relationship. The relationship must come first or it will not last.

Do what you can to help or to get help, but if the destructive behavior continues, the relationship will probably go through a long and painful path leading to its dissolution. The way to protect yourself and your relationship is to lay it on the line. If your mate values alcohol or drugs more than the relationship and you, it's better to end it quickly. Perhaps after it's over, your partner will stop drinking and be ready to resume the relationship. Sometimes it takes a firm drawing of boundaries to resolve such a situation. At Passages Addiction Cure Center, we always have several people in treatment whose partner has demanded that they get treatment.

Physical abuse: The same thing applies to physical abuse, which threatens not only the endurance of the relationship but also you or your family's safety. When someone is physically hurting you, that's a deal breaker. If you feel that you need punishment, see a psychologist and get therapy. You do not deserve to be harmed and there are healthier ways of moving past guilt and other painful emotions.

Mental and emotional abuse: Treat mental and emotional abuse in the same way as physical abuse. You must put an end to it. Love yourself. Honor yourself. Cherish yourself. That is how to cause your mate to honor and cherish you as well. Do not condemn yourself to a third-rate relationship by accepting disrespectful treatment. What you are after is a first-class, loving, respectful relationship and nothing else. Expect it, demand it, and go for it.

Infidelity: If your partner cheats on you and has sex with someone else, the trust is gone, the respect is gone, and it's unlikely that it will come back. Trust, once broken, can be restored under ideal circumstances and over a long period of time, but this is rarely the case. For almost everyone, it's a deal breaker. There may be other considerations, such as children, finances, physical dependency, family, and social implications. You have to weigh the various aspects involved in your situation and come to your own conclusion. If you do elect to continue the relationship, realize that you may be living with a third-class relationship for a long while. (In Law 12, you'll read more about the important factor of trust in a relationship.)

HOW MUCH OF YOURSELF DO YOU GIVE?

One of the obstacles to putting your relationship first is simply the challenge of giving your relationship the attention it needs. You have only so much attention to give. In these days of instant global communication, if you permit it, your attention will be pulled this way and that by distractions of every shape and size, most of which have no value at all to you. When you allow your mind to be filled with useless information, you neglect those in your immediate environment—your loved ones.

"Paying attention to what is close at hand," says the I Ching, "brings great progress and good fortune." In other words, cultivating one's own garden—paying attention to one's own family and loved ones—is of much greater value than concentrating on the activities of some celebrity, political figure, or fascinating event. While those things may be interesting, in reality they have little or nothing to do with your everyday life and with the values you hold most dear. Get real.

How much time, energy, and attention you give something shows how much you care for it. How much do you give to your relationship? The answer to that question has a lot to do with whether you are in the present moment when you are with your partner and how you treat those moments.

In the book *Stranger in a Strange Land,* the science-fiction classic by Robert Heinlein, there's a wonderful passage that talks about being in the moment. The book is about a human, Michael Valentine Smith, who was raised on Mars and returns to Earth as a young adult. He has to learn about Earth's customs and culture, has never seen a woman before, and has many exceptional abilities that he learned on Mars. At one point in the story, a main character in the book asks one of the women Michael has kissed why it was so extraordinarily special to her. She dreamily explains that "Mike gives a kiss his whole attention." She says that most men, no matter how hard they try, have a part of their minds on something else, whether it's catching the next bus or worrying about their jobs, money, or what the neighbors might be saying. "But when Mike kisses you," she says, "he isn't doing anything else. Not anything. You're his whole universe for that moment."

That little lesson from Heinlein's novel can be applied to all the moments in your relationship. It's saying the same thing that all the enlightened sages have tried to tell us in every way they can: be fully present at every moment, be *with this moment.* It's also true that when you bring 100 percent of yourself to anything, you create the finest circumstances possible for it to thrive.

There's a popular children's song called "The Hokey Pokey." The singers all join hands and form a circle. Their actions follow the words of the song, which go something like this: "You put your left foot in, you put your left foot out, you put your left foot in, and you shake it all about." Later on, you put in your right foot, your right hand, until finally your whole self is in. Think about that song in terms of your relationship.

How much of yourself do you put in to your relationship? Do you only put your left foot in and then sit there wondering why you are getting less from the relationship than you want? Whatever you bring to the game of your life sets the limit for how much you can get out of life. To have the best, bring the best that you have.

THE POWER OF
PRIORITY

*The key is not to prioritize what's on your schedule,
but to schedule your priorities.*

~ STEPHEN COVEY (1932–)

To have an enduring and satisfying relationship, you must renew your commitment to maintaining that kind of relationship each time you think of your goal. That is what true commitment is. It constantly renews itself until the goal is fulfilled, the destination reached. When you are capable of that kind of commitment, you can reach any goal and arrive at any destination. Here are some questions that can help you focus on the all-important quality of endurance in your relationship:

~ Do I make important decisions in my life based on the survival of my relationship, or do I make

decisions based primarily on my own needs and
desires?

~ Have I ever had to make a serious choice
between something I wanted and something
my relationship partner said they wanted?
What choice did I make and what were the
consequences?

~ Is my relationship with my loved one a priority
in my life? How do I show my loved one that
our relationship is more important to me than
anything else?

~ What can I do to give more quality time, energy,
and attention to nurturing my relationship and
my loved one?

LAW 11

HARMONY STRENGTHENS,
DISHARMONY WEAKENS

*Many marriages would be better
if the husband and wife clearly understood
that they're on the same side.*

~ ZIG ZIGLAR (1926–)

We've all experienced how inner conflict can cause us to hesitate when it is time to act or move forward. Conflict within a marriage or partnership is the same. It will prevent those in the partnership from acting as a unit and meeting difficulties. When two people, be they partners, lovers, husband and wife, or participants in any other relationship attain sufficient depth in their relationship so that complete trust, understanding, and harmony reign, they will be able to undertake any goal, confront any danger, survive any hardship, and reach the heights of success without a misstep.

LAW II

HARMONY STRENGTHENS, DISHARMONY WEAKENS

AT THE BEGINNING OF THIS BOOK, I QUOTED Confucius saying that "when two people are at one in their inmost hearts, they shatter even the strength of iron or of bronze." That is because harmony strengthens and conflict weakens.

The word *harmony* comes from the Greek word *harmonia,* meaning joining, agreement, and concord of sounds. When harmony prevails, you do indeed have a "sound" relationship. Unresolved conflict, on the other hand, weakens the power to conquer danger without, whether that danger is physical or emotional or whether it comes from challenges to your livelihood, health, or even your very survival.

In business, disharmony results in a stressful workplace and ineffectiveness. In a family, disharmony results in a stressful home and in a poor living environment, making it difficult for the family to flourish. In any type of partnership or organization, disharmony is crippling. Constant disharmony in a relationship cripples not only the relationship but also each person in the relationship, just as harmony in a relationship empowers and strengthens each partner. To undertake great projects—and there is no greater project than a relationship—there must be unity, for it is only with unity that a concentrated, concerted effort toward any goal can be made.

You may think of disharmony as arguments or nasty fights, but it is much more than that. The ongoing little criticisms and snap judgments, sarcastic putdowns, and belittling comments can put up walls between you and your partner and harm a relationship even more than a stormy eruption that blows over quickly.

Another way that conflict weakens is that power struggles sap us of the energy we could be using not only to nurture the relationship but to nurture and strengthen ourselves. Chinese sages who lived thousands of years ago said it is unwise to obtain anything by force, for that which is obtained by force must be held by force.

The sages went on to say that it is a law of the

Universe that whatever you obtain by force, even though it may appear to temporarily benefit you, will ultimately bring you unhappiness in one form or another.

If you constantly pressure your spouse or partner so that every issue that arises comes out in your favor—whether it's deciding what to do on a day off or how to spend money—you are, in effect, obtaining your goal by force. The constant exertion it takes to hold anything by force, including forcing your will on others, drains your energy, invites the censure of others, and inevitably leads to regret.

How You View Disagreements

Being in harmony does not mean that you will not or should not have disagreements. These are part of life and part of every relationship. How you view or resolve your disagreements is what makes the difference.

One thing that can help you resolve conflicts is to remember that when you and your partner quarrel, you are actually seeking harmony, although it may not appear so. You are trying to mold the other person into a form you are compatible with, and vice versa. In actuality, arguing is trying to find balance in an unbalanced manner. Quarreling is an unrefined, unsophisticated way to achieve harmony and come to an agreement; but if you have not learned a better way, that is all that is left to you. Rather than aggressively arguing, try to use the conflicts that arise as opportunities to listen with your heart to what is going on below the surface.

Do not be one of those people who let their arguments flame out of control because you lack the discipline to calmly and lovingly discuss a situation. Both you and your partner are seeking balance, seeking to have each other see it your way. Communication is a skill, and you can learn to communicate calmly, seeking always to communicate with love in your voice. Keep love alive. Do not win an argument at the expense of your relationship.

Learn to simply overlook the little faults of your loved one, the failings and shortcomings. Review Law 4 on Safe Space. You and your partner have idiosyncrasies and quirks, but they do not define who either of you are. Those quirks are small compared to the wondrous gifts and potentials each of you possesses.

GENEROSITY OF HEART

Another way to achieve harmony in a relationship is to be generous of heart rather than stingy and hurtful. When you embody the characteristics of generosity and kindness, by the Law of Cause and Effect you will find your own world filled with those who are generous and kind.

Ancient wisdom teaches, "Through hardness and selfishness, the heart grows rigid, and this rigidity leads to separation from others." When those you love are in need and you turn away from them, that is the beginning of hardness. If they ask you for help and you selfishly hoard your time and energy, refusing to share yourself with them, the hardness grows and soon you begin to look at them from behind a mask of hardness. That mask separates you from your loved ones. Who wants to be around someone who is cold and ungiving?

Hardness and selfishness, gentleness and generosity—they each bring their own inevitable results. That is especially true in relationships, where we are literally "joined together." When you are in a relationship, joined as one, what you do and feel, how you act and react affects you both, for good or for ill.

In essence, generosity leads to living, stinginess to dying. Love leads to living, hate to dying. It's actually a very simple equation. Relationships where continued conflict and tension exist, where the partners withhold the best part of themselves from each other, are not living relationships; they are relationships in the process of dying. To preserve what you have, to keep your relationships alive and glowing, give generously—give of your time, your assets, your attention, your help, and your love. Give of yourself.

THE POWER OF GENTLE GENEROSITY

Opposition brings concord.
Out of discord comes the fairest harmony.

~ HERACLITUS OF EPHESUS (CA. 540 BC – CA. 480 BC)

Our disagreements can often be about our unmet needs or unresolved inner conflicts. Sometimes our real needs are hidden underneath our hurts. When disharmony arises, it can be a hidden blessing—the means of uncovering and healing what's festering under the surface. Here are three simple steps you can try the next time a disagreement arises. Rather than reacting defensively when you or a loved one feels hurt or upset, use a gentle, generous approach:

~ Stop.
~ Take a few deep breaths.
~ Then simply ask your partner what they need from you.

At times, your loved one may not know the answer to that question. We don't always know what's bothering us. By being open to asking, "What do you need?" you are helping your partner discover the answer to that question. You are helping your partner reflect on what is really happening inside of them. If you act gently and wisely, rather than responding aggressively with your ego, your disagreements can be golden opportunities for discovery.

LAW 12

An Ideal Relationship Can Only Exist within Complete Trust

Dare to be true: nothing can need a lie.

~GEORGE HERBERT (1593 – 1633)

Trust is the greatest of all the foundations on which to build your relationship. Trust makes it possible for you to tell your partner your deepest fears, greatest shames, and most private thoughts without fear of ridicule or misunderstanding. Trust permits you both to soar free, roaming the skies of love without fear of falling. Without complete trust, there can be no first-class relationship. It is better not to have a relationship at all than to exist in a condition of dishonor and distrust and to share a relationship that is less than all it could be.

LAW 12

AN IDEAL RELATIONSHIP CAN ONLY EXIST WITHIN COMPLETE TRUST

A MODERN-DAY PARABLE BY AN ANONYMOUS AUTHOR gives a wonderful lesson about trust. One day, a little girl and her father were crossing a bridge. They had been out walking, and it was getting dark when they reached a narrow bridge over a rushing stream. The father was concerned for his daughter's safety and didn't want her to be scared. So he turned to her and said, "Sweetheart, please hold my hand so that you don't fall into the river."

The little girl said, "No, Dad. You hold my hand."

"What's the difference?" asked the puzzled father. "There's a big difference," replied the little girl. "If I hold your hand and something happens to me, I may let go of your hand. But if *you* hold *my* hand, I know for sure that no matter what happens, you will never let go of my hand."

It's a wonderful feeling when you can trust someone like that. It's a feeling of complete security, knowing you can totally depend on that person.

TRUTHFULNESS AND
FIRST-CLASS RELATIONSHIPS

It takes years to build trust, but only a moment to destroy it. The first time a lie escapes your lips or the lips of your partner, or the first time you are untrue to each other, you have condemned yourselves to a second-class relationship.

Truthfulness is *truth-fullness*. That means "all the truth, all the time." No secrets, no distortion of facts, no lies, and no fibs (which are small distortions of the truth, but lies nevertheless). Telling the truth also means no omissions. There must be absolute certainty in your minds that you can completely trust one another and that neither of you is holding anything back. Be brave enough to tell your partner everything, not omitting anything. It takes courage, but you can summon enough courage to face even your greatest fear.

There are times when your very survival may depend on the trustworthiness of your spouse or partner. People have had to trust each other with their very lives. That's the kind of trust I'm writing about here—"to die for" trust. There may well come make-it or break-it times in your relationship when it is crucial that you or your loved one be able to rely totally on each other's word. Perhaps one of you is accused of something by a third person that could be a deal breaker for a relationship if it were true. At that moment, there must exist such absolute trust that the accused party simply has to say, "That's not true," and that's the end of it.

I'm not talking about putting on a good face and sticking up for your mate even though you might suspect there is some truth in the accusation. Having 100 percent trust in your partner means that you know in your heart of hearts that what your partner is telling you is the truth. There is such security and oneness in that feeling that it will outweigh nearly every fault your partner might have. Millennia ago, the great poet Homer wrote in his classic *The Odyssey* these words that still hold true today: "May heaven grant you in all things your heart's desire—husband, house, and a happy, peaceful home; for there is nothing better in this world than that man and wife should be of one mind in a house. It discomfits their enemies [and] makes the hearts of their friends glad."

You and your loved one also need to trust each other to *be* a certain way. You both need to know that when you are not together, each of you is acting the part of a faithful, loving, respectful partner in a lifelong partnership. You need to be able to trust one other not to flirt with others, to always conduct yourselves as if you were together, never to say anything to someone that you would not say if your partner were present, and to keep uppermost in your minds that you are in a wonderful, loving, trusting, permanent relationship. When you are part of a relationship, what you do affects and reflects on your partner. Trustworthy partners always think first before they do anything that may affect either the reputation or well-being of each other.

When Trust Disappears

When trust disappears, the implications are enormous. Losing faith in your partner can be devastating and easily end a relationship. At Passages Addiction Cure Center, some of those who come to us for help in recovering from alcoholism or addiction have just learned that their spouse was cheating on them. Usually their faces are pale from the shock of it. The question they ask is: "How could they have done that to me?" They can't get their minds around the terrible deception. It's as if their world has just dissolved around them, and, in fact, it has. They had constructed a world built on trust, and suddenly the trust was gone, and along with it their relationship.

All their plans and all the details of their days were based on their relationship, and the news that their spouse has cheated on them is devastating. Sometimes the breakup happens many years into the marriage, and they feel as if the marriage was an illusion, their relationship a fraud. One woman told me, "I feel as if my whole marriage of twenty-five years has been a sham."

Even if the relationship doesn't end because of the betrayal, the core of it can be ruined, and to deal with the wreckage that's left is very difficult. It's doubly hard if children are involved because they, too, lose trust in their parent and are left adrift, wondering what else they can't depend on. In most cases, distrust is instilled in their minds and it will take a great deal of work in the future to reverse it.

I've seen others at Passages who have discovered that their spouse told a white lie of some sort. Maybe a husband thought it was harmless to tell his wife he was working late when we was really joining friends at a bar. Or maybe a wife kept from her husband the truth that she was using money they had saved to buy something personal for herself. Even in the case of these white lies, we see the results of the loss of trust, and I can tell you that people are shattered by it. They start asking themselves: "What else was I lied to about? What else don't I know? Can I fully trust this person ever again?" In many cases, the breaking of trust was what drove people to turn to drugs or alcohol in the first place.

There are other subtle but powerful repercussions from telling your partner or spouse a lie. First, you know it. That creates a red flag in your mind and you have to be careful from that point onward lest you forget your lie and say something that will reveal the truth. You have to live a constant lie, being ever on guard in case you make a slip. Keeping up a pretense is not only tiresome, but it also creates a poor self-image, which, as I talked about earlier, can prevent you from having a healthy relationship.

The consequence of constant deception is that you will see yourself as a liar, a deceiver; and who you *think* you are permeates everything else you do. It becomes part of your self-image. Having a tarnished self-image reduces your chances of having a great relationship because in order to have a first-class relationship, you must deserve it, and more than that, you must *believe* you deserve it.

Don't underestimate the power of this concept. Your self-image and your character are among the most valuable tools you have for building the relationship of your dreams. Knowing that you are worthy and believing that you deserve a great relationship are key factors in creating that kind of relationship. If you believe you deserve a first-class relationship, you will not settle for anything less. And if your mate isn't treating you with the respect and consideration you believe you deserve, you will take action to address their conduct and remedy the situation. What you believe about yourself empowers you to take action on your own behalf.

Pretending Only Brings Hurt

If you are in a relationship and have already been less than completely truthful with your partner, you can still remedy this situation by making your partner aware of your untruthfulness and of your intention to be honorable in the future. You may fear that if your partner hears the truth from you, it will end your relationship. That's a possibility. What's worse, though, is either having your loved one find out that you've lied or having to live the lie. In both cases, the trust is gone, and with it the chance of having a great relationship.

A friend once admitted to me that he had been unfaithful to his wife. When I suggested to him that he be truthful and tell her of his infidelity, he told me, "She couldn't handle the truth." The fact is that he was the one who couldn't handle the truth. He was afraid of the consequences of the truth. He was afraid that his wife would leave him if she found out he had been unfaithful to her. So they were forced to live a lie, existing in a relationship where there was no trust. As a result, their relationship went from bad to worse and ended in divorce. Like all false illusions, pretending only brings hurt and despair to everyone.

What if you feel that a partner's breach of trust is so severe that your relationship cannot be repaired and you want to end it? Say, for instance, you discover that your partner is having an affair with one of your close friends. The news is crushing. You feel humiliated, broken, used, and angry. Your partner has broken the spoken or unspoken vows the two of you made when you entered into the relationship and has shown himself or herself to be unworthy of your love and trust. How should you respond?

First wait. Do not do anything in the heat of anger or hurt. As the saying goes, "Act in haste and repent at leisure." Passion and reason cannot exist together. When anger, lust, or hatred consumes you, clear, rational thinking is impossible. It is only when you are able to calmly step back from yourself and "look in on yourself " that true detachment can be achieved, which then permits rational thinking. Step back from the situation and carefully consider what action to take. Your next steps will most likely be life altering.

If you do decide that your partner's behavior is a deal breaker, before you break up, plan carefully. There is much at stake here and many considerations that come into play, including children, finances, families, religion, and other values that may be important to you. If no children, finances, or other major considerations are involved, it's just a question of whether or not you want to be in a relationship with someone you can't trust.

There can be an upside to the relationship challenges you face, which is why it's important not to act in haste. Not only can a challenge teach you much about your partner, but it can also teach much about yourself. It can help you clarify for yourself what is essential to you in a relationship and what is a deal breaker so that you can define and stand up for your needs. The challenge can also be a wake-up call that shows both of you where you need to make adjustments in your own character to preserve your relationship and your love. Challenges often reveal where there are cracks in the foundation so you can repair those weaknesses and build a stronger foundation that will last through the years.

SHARING YOUR HOPES AND DREAMS

Trust isn't automatic in a relationship. It's something that is built over time. In the beginning of a relationship, you may have little trust because you don't yet know each other or you may have been lied to, cheated, betrayed, or had your trust shattered at different times in your life. It's at the beginning of a relationship that you are faced with the great potential of building your partnership based on perfect trust. That's the time to establish the habit of trust as well as the habit of opening yourself up and sharing with each other your deepest hopes and dreams—who you are and who you want to become.

I have been keenly aware of that in my own life. About twenty-five years ago, I was in between relationships and was hoping for the longed-for person to show up. I was actually apprehensive should the woman of my dreams appear, because in my younger days I had difficulty breaking the ice with new female acquaintances and it had carried over into my later years. As I sat in front of my fire one evening musing about the difficulty, I wrote something that expressed what I felt about trust, commitment, and discovery within a relationship.

Years later, I met that someone I had been hoping to meet—my wife, Lyn. You read earlier how we met. After I left Kauai, Lyn and I communicated by phone and email for several months. At one point, I felt compelled to email Lyn what I had written that evening years ago as I had sat before my fire in the hope that it would convey to her more of who I am. I share it with you because it's true of all first meetings. And it's about opening yourself at any stage of your relationship to the hopes, the fears, and the dreams that you bring with you into your partnerships.

It's called "Out of Context," and it's about preparing to meet someone for the first time, someone you think might be "The One."

Out of Context
We are about to meet, you and I, my new
love, and I am afraid to speak—afraid that
I will not be able to communicate myself to
you, for anything I say will be "out of context." And how could it be otherwise? You do
not know and have not experienced the journey of my life—my hopes and fears, what I
hold dear, whose thoughts I venerate, the stuff
of which I'm made. You do not know of my
triumphs and my failures, my joys and heartbreaks, the times I have risen to overcome

seemingly insurmountable obstacles, the times I have been overcome by them.

You do not know the tenacity of my spirit. You do not know I can endure to the end of even the greatest travail. You are unaware that I can help you raise your consciousness so you can become the ultimate woman you can be, the woman you've always struggled to be, the woman you want the world, or at least me, to know you as.

Words I use may have a different meaning for you than they do for me. You may not hear my real meaning, the deeper meaning of which my soul is speaking. If I speak of trust, you may not know I mean "to die for" trust. If I speak of courage, you may not know that I mean "to prevail in the face of even the greatest danger possible." The stuff of the Universe flows through my heart, veins, and mind, as it does in yours.

So I hope you will be patient with me while the subtle being within you begins to sense the deeper currents of my being, causing you to wait while who I am unfolds. I can be

great, bold, courageous, tender, caring, intuitive. I can speak words of wisdom gathered in
the fields, mountains, cities, bedrooms, and
boardrooms where I have met and conquered
my fears and endured my trials.

I can caress the most tender strands of
your being, causing them to vibrate in the
ecstasy of being touched by one who under-
stands your soul. I can open you to the secrets
of your heart and lift your spirits wonderfully
high.

So many have passed by, only look-
ing with their eyes to see if I was the one for
whom they were searching, not knowing that
the person in whom they would be interested
could only be perceived with their hearts and
minds after a long excursion down the path
with me. We are two people meeting on the
shores of their souls, each hoping the other
will perceive the continents that lie within.

So come, let us now partake of each
other, my new love. Look, here I am, walking
toward you, but "out of context." We meet, we
pause, we look, hesitating. Now I gather my

courage, now I speak to you, hoping you will understand... "Hello..."

Some months later, Lyn and I were married. At our wedding, she asked me to read what I had written to the assembled guests. The two of us began the long journey down the path with each other, full of trust, full of love, confident in each other.

The exercise of writing this piece years ago helped me express what was in my heart. It helped me articulate and clarify my hopes and dreams, be honest with myself, and, as importantly, be honest and open with my wife to be.

THE POWER OF
TRUTH AND TRUST

*Nothing gives such a blow to friendship as
the detecting another in an untruth; it strikes
at the root of our confidence ever after.*

~ WILLIAM HAZLITT (1778–1830)

First-class relationships are possible only in an atmosphere of total trust. To trust, as dictionaries define it, is to rely on someone and to place yourself in his or her care. What does trust really look like in a relationship, apart from the need to remain faithful? Here are some questions to help you reflect on trust and how you can become more trustworthy.

~ Am I trustworthy? Can my partner rely on me to do what I say I am going to do?

~ Am I truthful to my partner? Do I tell the truth and not withhold facts?

~ Can my partner trust me to provide unconditional support—physically, mentally, emotionally, even spiritually—in all circumstances?

~ Can my partner trust that I will be open to whatever my partner tells me and that I won't judge, laugh, or dismiss their concerns, fears, and innermost feelings?

~ Likewise, am I honest and open about how I feel, not hiding my doubts, fears, or feelings from my partner?

~ When my partner is absent, can I be trusted to talk to others about my partner with support and appreciation and never critically or disparagingly?

~ Do I see myself and my partner as a team, never taking an action or saying anything that would affect their well-being or reputation or undermine their potential to blossom?

~ What can I do to increase the trust my partner has in me?

LAW 13

Every Action Produces a Result That Is in Exact Accord with the Action

There is only one constant,
one universal. It is the only real truth:
Causality. Action, reaction. Cause and effect.

~ Merovingian, *The Matrix Reloaded*

Every moment that you are interacting with others, you are creating effects. Every moment that you are interacting with your loved one, you are creating effects in your relationships. As a direct result of your interactions, your relationship is either flourishing or disintegrating. That is how the Law of Cause and Effect works, and it is unerring. As Ralph Waldo Emerson put it, "Cause and effect are two sides of one fact." Once you understand the Law of Cause and Effect more fully, it will become one of the greatest tools in your relationship tool bag.

LAW 13

EVERY ACTION PRODUCES A RESULT THAT IS IN EXACT ACCORD WITH THE ACTION

THE METAPHYSICAL (BEYOND THE PHYSICAL) LAW OF Cause and Effect states that every action produces a reaction that is in exact accord with the action that caused it. (Please do not think that this is the same as the physical law of cause and effect, which states that every action produces an equal and opposite reaction.) The metaphysical Law of Cause and Effect is happening all around you all the time. The happy person and the cheerless person have arrived at their respective states of mind as the direct result of their prior conduct. If you are angry much of the time, you will have few friends, it will be hard for you to succeed in business, and the possibility of having even a poor relationship is nearly nonexistent. If, on the other hand, you are cheerful, forgiving, and patient, you will find yourself living in quite a different world as you reap the results of your open-heartedness.

The Feedback Loop

In actuality, you've been reading about the Law of Cause and Effect throughout this book as you've discovered how living in accord with each of the Laws of Love will bring positive results in your relationship—and how not doing so will create difficulty and division between you and your loved one. One important way you can become attuned to how causes you have set in motion manifest in your relationship is to start to see the world you live in, the world of cause and effect, as a dynamic world in the truest sense of the word. To be dynamic is to be active, changing, full of energy and purpose, and making progress. That progress takes place because there is a continuous feedback loop between you and the Universe—*because the Universe is continually conscious and totally aware of you.*

It's critically important that you grasp this concept and its implications if you are to fully understand and work with the Law of Cause and Effect to create happy and fulfilling relationships. Let's start with the idea that everything in the Universe is made of the same energy. Currently, the world's most famous equation is Albert Einstein's $E=mc^2$. It means that E (energy) equals m (mass) multiplied by c (the velocity of light) squared. In effect, this equation tells us that *energy* and the *physical matter* of the Universe, including you and me, are different forms of the same thing. Not only is that true, but you are part of the same energy that is the entire Universe. In other words, you *are* the Universe—an inseparable part of it.

The word *Universe* is made up of two Latin words, *uni* (meaning "one") and *versus* (from the root word meaning "to turn"). Literally, it can be taken to mean "one turned into." You can think of the "one" as a vast body of conscious energy that turned itself into the multitude of things that make up "the Universe," including you. That is not so different from the common belief in most religions, perhaps all religions, that in the beginning there was a supreme being, a God (who is referred to by thousands of names), who created the heavens and the earth. That's why I capitalize the word *Universe.*

I believe not only that we are part of the Universe but that we share in its consciousness. Our consciousness is part of the Universal consciousness. It's like a light bulb. When you screw in the bulb to the electrical socket, it begins to partake of the electricity that is coursing through the wires. The electricity does not originate in the bulb, just as your consciousness does not originate in your brain. You partake of the field of consciousness that exists in the Universe. The Universe knows everything there is to know about you and loves you completely—because *you* are *it*.

Here's the next piece of information that will help you understand how Universal consciousness works and assist you in making the changes that are so vitally important in the building of your relationship. Since you are part of the Universe, it can communicate with you, and you with it. How? You speak to the Universe with words, thoughts, and actions, and the Universe speaks to you with events.

Events are the language of the Universe. An example of an event is what we call coincidence, although there is actually no such thing in the Universe. A meeting "by chance" is not actually by chance but by design. Every event is a Universal communication.

The Universe brings events into your life to guide you, instruct you, and also deter you from a course of action that would not be in your best interest so that you can grow and learn and create yourself as a perfect human. So when things are or are not going well in your relationship, you are, in effect, receiving a communication from the Universe, a response to your actions that is giving you feedback—new information you need so you can clearly see the results of your thoughts, attitudes, behavior, and actions.

Perhaps that communication comes through the words or behavior of your partner or through other people and situations that weave their way through your life. By learning to read and interpret those event communications, you can get valuable information that can put you back on the path of a resilient relationship if you make the adjustments that are called for.

Another key to understanding the Law of Cause and Effect, one that can be a real life-changer, is this: by acknowledging that the Universe is communicating with you through events and circumstances—with just a little knowing smile, a nod of your head, a thumbs-up signal—the Universe becomes aware that you are aware of it and therefore raises the level of communication. When that happens, you can make more progress more quickly. To be aware that the Universe is constantly communicating with you is to live in a manner only to be thought of as magical, and it brings rewards of ever-greater significance.

Know the Seeds

Learning to detect the communications that come to you, in subtle or direct ways, is invaluable in relationships. Long before the avalanche cascades down the hill, minute, imperceptible changes have been progressing in the earth. Good fortune and misfortune both have their respective beginnings long before they become evident. The same is true in our relationships. It's important to know the seeds.

You can always sense when things are not going well in your relationship. Have you ever watched an animal in the wild, or seen one in a film, that senses danger—how it stands absolutely still, head up, ears cocked to perceive any danger? That's how you must be in your relationship.

Be alert to the subtle shifting of the relationship winds, and take action to prevent your relationship from going off course. A little thoughtfulness when you first sense a change in the current of your relationship will bring great blessings. That is a time when small efforts bring large rewards.

Unlike formal relationships where the duties and rights of the participants are set forth in written documents, relationships of the heart depend on the consideration and thoughtfulness of the partners and on their affection for one another. In personal relationships, affection and consideration are the main ingredients. Each act of kindness shows your loved one that you value and appreciate him or her.

When we fail to treat our loved ones with the simplest kindness, opportunities to show our love and build the foundations of a magnificent relationship slip through our fingers. The American poet Stephen Vincent Benét put it this way:

> Life is not lost by dying! Life is lost
> Minute by minute, day by dragging day,
> In all the thousand, small, uncaring ways.

THE POWER OF
SMALL ACTS OF KINDNESS

*What and how we will be in the future
depends on what we do now.*

~ DAISAKU IKEDA (1928–)

One way you can begin to work consciously with the Law of Cause and Effect is simply to create a list of the things you know will make your partner happy. Each day, add one of those things to your to-do list and do it. You don't have to do something huge. Sometimes the small acts of kindness touch another's heart the most deeply. And don't think of it as a chore. Think of it as a priority for keeping your love and relationship alive. By doing at least one special thing a day for your partner, taking time to bring happiness to the one you care for most, you are sowing seeds that will bear fruit.

I've listed below just a few ideas of the kinds

of items you can add to your list of things that will make your partner happy. They are not necessarily novel ideas, and you will certainly think of many more ideas tailored to your partner's specific needs and personality. I list these here to show you that it isn't hard to find one thing to do each day to bring happiness to the one you love. Revisit your list often and add new items to it.

~ Give compliments. That is very important.

~ Acknowledge thoughtful acts.

~ Remember special occasions.

~ Be helpful whenever the opportunity presents itself.

~ Find ways to improve your immediate environment.

~ Do something unexpected that brings happiness.

~ Give regular ten-minute foot rubs, massages, scalp rubs, back scratches.

~ Help out with other chores normally done by your mate.

~ Be supportive.

~ Be a good listener, and know when to remain silent.

~ Don't always insist on having your way.

~ Give a gift, even something small, such as a favorite snack or food, a flower, a CD of music, a DVD you can watch together, a loofah mitt for the bath, a book on a topic your partner is interested in, a note on the pillow, a suggestion for an evening out together or a movie night, a little poem you have written, a package of incense, or a framed picture of the two of you together or of parents, siblings, or friends.

~ And, of course, being happy and upbeat as much as you can is one of the greatest gifts you can give anyone.

LAW 14

You Are the Author
of Every Next Moment

How am I going to live today *in order
to create the tomorrow I'm committed to?*

~ANTHONY ROBBINS (1960–)

Now that you understand the Law of Cause and Effect, there is one more piece to put in place that will help you create a strong personal philosophy and use all the Laws of Love in this book to create your ideal relationship. It is this: *you are the author of every next moment of your life.* You are in control of how you will react and respond at any given moment. In fact, you are far more powerful than you suspect because you are the center of your personal Universe.

LAW 14

YOU ARE THE AUTHOR
OF EVERY NEXT MOMENT

YOU MAY NOT THINK OF YOURSELF AS BEING THE center of *the* Universe, and most likely you're not. Yet there is a universe where you are the key player and where you are the center. I call it your "personal Universe." It is that portion of the Universe that affects you personally and that you affect.

Every time you speak or act in any manner, you are affecting everything in your personal Universe. If you assist someone and years later that person does you a favor, you have affected your personal Universe and have been affected by it. If you hurt your mate physically, emotionally, or spiritually and they react by emotionally closing down or getting angry, you are experiencing the effects of causes you have set in motion in your personal Universe. Whatever you perceive by hearing, seeing, touching, smelling, or tasting is coming to you from your personal Universe.

You are the command center, receiving information and taking actions.

Your personal Universe exists *only* because you exist. If you didn't exist, neither would your personal Universe. In that Universe, you *are* the center. Being the center of your personal Universe is more than being *at* the center. If you were only at the center, when you moved, you would move away from the center. *Being the center* means that as you move, the center moves with you.

Only when you are fully aware that you are the center of your personal Universe—creating and influencing everything around you by being how you're being at every moment—will you understand the importance of your every thought and act, and how it creates or destroys your happiest relationship.

You Are Capable of Fulfilling Your Goals

The concept that you are creating your relationship on a moment-by-moment basis may take a bit of getting used to, but the effort you put into it will pay huge dividends. If it's hard to imagine yourself as the center of your personal Universe, think of it this way. Imagine your life as a movie where you've been cast as the hero. Take a moment to look back on the last year or even the last month of your life. Have you been a good hero? Have you been the kind of person you would like others to see and emulate? Have you been the kind of person who would attract the love and devotion of the one you want to share your life with?

Guess who is the director of that movie? Who's the producer? Who's the main actor? Who's the script writer? If you don't like the script or the direction the movie is going in, who has the power to change it? You do, because you are the author of every next moment of your life.

As you've been reading this book and learning about the Laws of Love, you've probably identified some changes you would like to make. If the task seems overwhelming, don't let that stop you. You cannot cultivate a huge field all at once, but by plowing one furrow at a time you will inevitably see the entire field cultivated.

To contemplate an entire trek up a great mountain is daunting. However, one step up the mountain is easy to take, and so follow the rest of the steps until the summit is reached. In the same way, it's difficult to envision a year's worth of changes or an entire project from the start. But if you break the year or the project down into months, then days, then hours, you can master the visioning. Know that whatever has occurred before, whatever your current circumstances may be, whatever dreams you have for your life and your relationships, you are perfectly equipped and fully capable of fulfilling your goals and desires—one step at a time.

THE POWER OF
THE NEXT STEP

*If one advances confidently in the direction of his dreams,
and endeavors to live the life which he has imagined, he will
meet with a success unexpected in common hours.*

~ HENRY DAVID THOREAU (1817–1862)

When you start working with the Laws of Love, you need not be overly concerned about the outcome. All that is necessary is that you begin. Start with small, easily handled tasks, one step at a time. Remember that the Universe is always aware of you and will respond to you as you take the next step. Each small, positive change you make will affect your partner and your relationship for the better.

~ Focus on one Law of Love at a time. Review the chapter on that law as well as the suggested action steps that follow it. Think about how that law applies to your specific relationship or the relationship you want to see in your life.

~ Identify one thing you can do to work with that law to bring about positive results.

~ Once you have a feel for how that law works and can see some results in your life, you can add new action steps that relate to that Law of Love or go on to the next law.

As you focus on each law, you will start to perceive events, yourself, and your partner in a new way. Seeing in that new way will lead you to respond in a new way. And as a result of natural law, the Law of Cause and Effect, you *will* create new results in your life.

That is not to say that you won't have challenges. Yet even in the most difficult times that test your relationship, you will have confidence in yourself and in the future because you have the tools you need— you will know how to work within the Laws of Love. All that is necessary for you to achieve success, great success, is to have the determination to reach your goals, cultivate endurance as an established trait of character, and follow the path of the Laws of Love.

In Conclusion

The Laws of Love are unbreakable, unchangeable, everlasting. You can depend on them. Trust what you have read. Give it your all, holding back nothing. Bring all of yourself to living life and loving. You are a golden being in a deathless Universe, destined to be here at this magical moment in time where you can have the relationship of your dreams, and better. I wish you golden moments, treasured times, and an abundance of love.

Olivia

I Ching Workbook
The entire text of *The I Ching: The Book of Answers*
and 100 workbook pages to record your answers
By Wu Wei, Trade Paperback

I Ching Workbook Deluxe Gift Set
The entire text of *The I Ching: The Book of Answers*
and 100 workbook pages to record your answers,
10" yarrow stalks, sandalwood incense, Auroshikha
incense holder, and silk I Ching cloth
By Wu Wei

I Ching Gift Set
The entire text of *The I Ching: The Book of Answers*
and 7" yarrow stalks
By Wu Wei

50 Yarrow Stalks from China
Handpicked by farmers in northeast China specifically
for use with the I Ching.
7" yarrow stalks (50)
10" yarrow stalks (50)

Published by Power Press
www.PowerPressPublishing.com

Bookstores, please contact SCB Distributors toll free at
800-729-6423 or 310-532-9400. Fax: 310-532-7001
E-mail: info@scbdistributors.com
Website: www.scbdistributors.com

For foreign and translation rights, contact Nigel J. Yorwerth
E-mail: nigel@PublishingCoaches.com

CHRIS PRENTISS is the author of several popular works on personal growth, including *Zen and the Art of Happiness; The Alcoholism and Addiction Cure; Be Who You Want, Have What You Want; The Little Book of Secrets;* and *The I Ching: The Book of Answers.* He is the cofounder of the world-renowned Passages Addiction Cure Centers. He has also written, produced, and directed a feature film. Chris Prentiss lives with his wife in Hawaii.